King Blue

Boogie Till The Roof Caves In

By Al Simmons

A Stone Wind Publication

Al Simmons

King Blue
Boogie Till The Roof Caves In
A Kingston Mines Journal

with Photographs by
D. Shigley
*(except photos on pages
64, 68 and 82).*

ISBN 0-9630849-0-9

Grateful acknowlegements to the editors of the following publications where portions of this book first appeared: The Chicago Reader, Fanatic Magazine & Rolling Stock.

Special thanks to Doc Pellegrino for years of friendship and the inside track necessary in order to make this book possible, and Terry Jacobus, for general inspiration, brotherhood, friendship and book design.

This book is dedicated to D. Shigley in memorium.

Copyright 1992
by Al Simmons and D. Shigley.
All rights reserved.

A Stone Wind Publication
6936 North Bell Street
Chicago, Illinois 60645

Preface

Ten years ago, when portions of this book began showing up in the print media, the preface to the story began thus: "At 5 a. m., last November 11, the roof of the building at 2354 N. Lincoln Avenue, home of the Kingston Mines for the past 12 years, collapsed; and with it went most of the building's second and third floors and half of the building's rear brick wall. Despite the absence of half a roof and most of the building's rear structure, the Kingston Mines was open for business the following night. The Skid City Blues Band, featuring Detroit Junior, inspired enough rocking and reeling to provoke calls from neighbors and visits from police who wanted to know what all the commotion was about. One might say the Kingston Mines boogied until the roof came down, then boogied a little more."

Now, as I sit here reviewing these pages for print once again, I am amazed how simply that single paragraph captured the spirit and heart that made the Kingston Mines - Chicago Blues Center, the largest and certainly the greatest showcase blues club in the world.

But back in the summer of 1979, when I first sat down and began to write this book, I was convinced, as I am now, that I was in the right place at the right time, and I had better record these stories because something very special was going on. What I did not anticipate was how that magic of the moment, and intensity I strived to record nearly ten years ago, could continue right on until today. And, as a matter of fact, the Kingston Mines today is bigger and better and far more successful than ever. And we can thank Doc Pellegrino, owner and impresario, for his ingenuity and drive in keeping the Kingston Mines alive. For anyone who has been around will assure you there is no place like Chicago, when it comes to the blues, and there is no place, for the blues, in Chicago, like the Kingston Mines.

Also, I would like to thank the estate of D. Shigley for allowing me to include his photographs in this edition, as D. Shigley and I had originally planned. Hope you enjoy the book.

Al Simmons
September 18, 1989
Berkeley, CA

King Blue
Boogie Till The Roof Caves In
A Kingston Mines Journal

An Opening Scenario *3*
Very Large Fish *5*
July, Friday The 13th, 1979 *8*
Doc Pellegrino *11*
Saturday Night, July 14, 1979 *15*
Monster Of The Blues Museum *18*
Monster, Part II *21*
Arrives The UnPress *24*
Pretences Of The Real World *26*
Friday Night, July 20, 1979 *31*
Tell Me, Why Do Young Men Go Wild? *35*
The Intimacy of Telepathy *40*
Not Fade Away *42*
The Inside Track *43*
La La La La La Bom-ba *45*
The Buddha Of Blues *47*
End Of The Day Revisited *49*
The Attack *50*
You Can Look At It This Way *51*
Scenario No. 23 *52*
Hounds In The Evening *(bitches in the night)* *55*
The Show Goes On *59*
Strictly Southside *61*
Dimestore Fred *63*
Blind Jim Brewer *65*
Johnny Dollar *69*
Armed To The Teeth *74*
These Guys Don't Care *76*
Speaking With Lefty Dizz *77*
King Azure Blue *83*

Living In Paradise *86*
Squeezing The Tail Of The Law *88*
A Pair Of Neon Eyebrows *90*
One Head Out The Door *92*
The Fact Of The Matter Is *94*
On The Price Of A Mythology *96*
Pie In The Sky *98*
Nuke Me Baby *(Nuke Me All Night Long)* *100*
Squared Black Holes *103*
But Dank Is Just A Word *105*
London During The Blitz *107*
News Spreads Fast *109*
Like A Hot Balloon In A Cold Cut Store *111*
A Liquid Of Amber Substance *113*
A Moral In The Story *117*
Like The Ancient Run Of The Caribou *121*
End Of The Season *123*
No Breaks *125*
Epilogue *128*

For Max and Clara

"Ingenuity is generosity transposed to the level of the intellect."

Claude Levi-Strauss

"It feels so good to bite the hook that hangs you."

Stephen J. Pantos

"The title of the song is *If you didn't jump out of the bushes and scare me, I never would have cut you.*"

Aron Burton

King Blue

Boogie Till The Roof Caves In

The Eddie Clearwater Blues Band, featuring "Big Bad" Leroy Brown

An Opening Scenario

The club is the Kingston Mines - Chicago Blues Center, owned by one Dr. Lenin Pellegrino, M. D., otherwise known as Doc, and located on north Lincoln Avenue at the Halsted/Fullerton triangle. It is summertime, 1979. Reportedly, the economy of America is failing. The President of the United States has taken up jogging. Our nation's foreign policy consists of carrying our allies and foreign occupations upon our shoulders like dandruff. In Washington, Presidential top official aides keep getting busted for drugs. Spills of radioactive waste and accidents at atomic power plants keep occuring everywhere. Yet, business at the Kingston Mines couldn't be better.

The house is packed to standing room only. The air is foul and thick with smoke. It is hot and sweaty and people are dancing and carrying on while a great show unfolds on stage.

The music is one long continuous set. It is the Eddie Clearwater Blues Band, featuring "Big Bad" Leroy Brown on vocals and tamborine, Lavelle White, Queen of the Kingston Mines, from Houston, Texas, blues buster woman on vocals, and Addie, a younger blond lady from Southern California, hard blues rocker brought to Chicago by Willie Dixon to cut an album, and playing exclusively in town for Doc.

The band begins its first set at 9:30 p.m. and plays till half past twelve. Takes a short twenty-five minute break, then plays straight on till 4 a.m. Somewhere in between Eddy Clearwater's songs and those of his three featured singers, during the second set, Syl Johnson, southside soul star and little brother to blues great, Jimmy Johnson, gets called up on stage to do a guest number or two, and asks the audience for requests.

"Let's hear some funk!" one guy from the audience calls out.

Syl Johnson calling back. "No, we don't play no funk here, man. This here is a blues bar."

"Nobody leave during the break now... cause we're coming back on with some shit so funky... they're gonna smell it down the street."

Phil Guy

Very Large Fish

A Sunday night benefit concert for the Walther Memorial Hospital, where Doc is medical chief of staff. 500 tickets presold. Hollow cool damp night. Doc's idea how to accommodate so many expected guests is to use the back room, which is a mess and has a broken sewer rancid damp smell hanging in the form of an actual vapor cloud due to a lack of ventilation in the incredible three story high cavern of the Mine's deep back interior. And the roof leaks.

Mary Hobbs, the Kingston Mines manager, and Doc's fiancée, has her crew rushing to get things done. The back door to the alley is pried open and the room is aired out. The refuge from the three large dogs, who live back there, is swept away and the concrete floor is hosed clean. A stage is set up, along with a make-shift service bar, while the tables and chairs, from the regular club, are brought in.

When the band arrives they set up a small light show consisting of two revolving lights, like squad car lights, one blue, one red, mounted overlooking the stage. The Phil Guy Blues Band, with featured vocalist, Lavelle White.

People began arriving out of the cold damp night. Maybe a slim hundred turned out in all. The music began. Really beautiful slicked down ladies with their gentlemen, dancing on the concrete floor.

Summertime. Outside it began raining. You could tell by the streams of water dripping down the back room walls, and the ensuing puddles of rain water growing on the dance floor. The damaged roof was leaking. While the band played, and the vapor cloud in the room began reforming, from the humidity and lack of ventilation. Too bad the large back doors to the alley had to be closed — the reason being the amplified sounds of the band would be too loud and disturbing to the neighbors. And the red and blue revolving lights became two beacons in the foggy sewer night.

And, oh yes, the sewer smell, along with the cloud, returning. Like dancing in a fish tank. Albeit, a very large fish tank. In a damp linen suit. With your favorite deep sea girl. Wondering if the fish tank filter had run amuck. Very subterranean. Takes on a certain sensory distortion. Like being on a foggy beach or pier and wondering what is going on. Except that you are not on a pier but in the extremely large back room of the Mines. And it is foggy. Which is no reason to end a party and no sensory distortion at all, but rather a physical environmental reality.

Yet, not a single verbal complaint was offered by patron, musician or management, at all. When the floor got too wet to dance, the people stopped dancing. When the room got too damp and uncomfortable to play, the band simply stopped playing. Then the night was over and everyone went home. A truly remarkable experience. The only descriptive comment I heard that night came from an ex-Korean War vet in Hawaiian shirt, getting drinks at the regular bar, in the un-fogged regularly used room, up front, said something like, "Hey man, battleship on the Indian Ocean." Right. As if he knew it.

Lefty Dizz

July, Friday The 13th, 1979

The house is packed for Lefty Dizz. It is 90 degrees hot outside, and humid, with multiple ozone pollution alerts. Big City. The evening begins with the beer cooler condensor going out, plus both air conditioners. The temperature in the club is about 105 degrees. There are no windows in the Kingston Mines, and now, with the air conditioners out, there is *no* longer any ventilation. The air quality in the smoke filled Mines rates with the air quality of quicksand. No one cares. Real bunch of survivors. Don't need fresh air. Like to sweat. Everyone calling out for Lefty Dizz, who is on the phone trying to reach his drummer who forgot to show up for the gig. Finally, Mary Hobbs finds someone in the audience who can play drums and is willing to fill in until the regular man shows up. The music has yet to begin and it is nearing 11 p.m. Lefty is at the bar calling out for a double Wild Turkey whiskey, straight up, to settle him down before he begins his set. Meanwhile, the audience is getting crazy. They are impatient, and hot, and rowdy, and drunk, and on their feet, and yelling, "Lefty! Lefty!"

Dizz flags down the bartender and tells him to, "Give me another shot....and I ain't got no money!"

The room has an air of the excited summer tourist. There are an unnatural number of Cadillac and Lincoln Towncars strewn about in the street, labelled with suburban township window stickers and out-of-state plates. All except for the new silver blue Cadillac Eldorado parked illegally out front blocking the street hydrant, which belongs to Lefty's bass player. And there is considerable interest as to how he got it. "Black Magic," is suggested.

Beer kegs are flowing like the River Nile Delta, Mississippi. The music finally begins. Lefty is completely raw and wild. He begins the set by mixing B. B. King lyrics to some music by Hound Dog Taylor, "Just to warm up," he says. Then pulls right into a tune by Lefty Dizz. Something about a one-eyed lady, who when her lover left her and her heart got broken, the pity was her tears only came out of one eye. "What a shame. What a shame." Then into an up tempo, "If I can just get my hands on/ what I got my eyes on/ oh, what a wonderful sight." While the audience is going crazy. Two hundred people up and dancing, peeling off their clothes and sweating, kicking loose and no longer caring about anything. Now with the room acclimated to the extreme heat, warm beer, and long wait. And the music finally playing. There are a few scattered tables and chairs broken, but not from anyone fighting. "It just broke," said one happy patron. It is all these people dancing.

Several couples in the crowd are wearing "Disco Sucks" tee shirts. There is a significant message there. A scene like this could never happen at a disco. There is nothing pre-recorded here. Which is the very reason, in fact, why these people are here and not down the street at a disco. They want it live. And they want to see Lefty Dizz do it live.

There is a report some gorilla just pulled a pipe out of the wall in the men's washroom, and a major flood is developing. The air conditioner suddenly flicks back on, for about twelve seconds, then goes off again. Not much. But just enough to let those paying attention know there is still some hope. The summer is only just beginning.

Doc Pellegrino and Margo Smith

Doc Pellegrino

Don't tell anyone but half the ladies working at the Kingston Mines are under age. Which is not any kind of new hiring program, but is more like a current trend. Though I can also recall a time when half the women working at the Kingston Mines had Ph.D.'s. But that was years ago when the Mines was busy being the last folk/rock club to survive the sixties, years before the Mines became the premier showcase blues club in Chicago. What makes the Kingston Mines so interesting is its owner, Doc Pellegrino. And, what makes Doc Pellegrino interesting is the fact that Doc is more than a night club owner. Doc Pellegrino is a benefactor. It is hard to think of anyone on the music side of Chicago's music industry who hasn't worked for him.

Doc, a native of Chicago, served in the 10th Mountain Division Ski Troops, and was twice wounded in combat. He is a general practitioner, with his private offices on West North Avenue in Chicago, and is Medical Chief-Of-Staff, and President of the Walther Memorial Hospital. He is an upright primate, about 50 years of age, 6'2", 210 lbs, father of five; two sons and three daughters, wears a full black beard, and carries a leather sap attached to the belt loop of his Lee Brand jeans.

Doc entered the business about fifteen years ago beginning with a coffee house in the suburbs, a place called Doc Gandolph's. There was some trouble at the time between the city officials of that suburb and a group of bikers that reached a climax one night in front of Doc's coffee house. Doc's club was cited as a meeting place for the gang, and although Doc beat the rap in court, and got rid of the loitering bikers, he decided the coffee house era was over and moved his interests into the city. Doc helped start Kingston Mines.

The Mines was originally established as two entities; a community theater where theatrical productions were produced in the cavernous-like back room. Where the nightclub is, was a restaurant/cafe/coffeehouse where young musicians sang and passed the hat. There was no alcohol being served then, and the food was ice cream, expresso coffee, teas, vegetarian cuisine. Walls have moved, the acts have changed. The club has seen its share of good days and bad days, tax collectors, frauds, etc., and minor financial miracles, which brings us to today.

But what has not changed, what Doc has maintained throughout the years at the Mines, is an on-going experiment and seeding bed for Chicago city culture. If you have an idea you can probably work it out at the Mines. The Broadway smash hit, "Grease", that was later filmed in Hollywood, was written and first produced in the back room of the Kingston Mines. There have been ragtime revivals, bluegrass festivals, folk extravaganzas, comedy showcases, a constant forum for poets, the first community theater in the area, a short term home for civil rights groups, anti-war groups, ERA groups, etc.. The list goes on. Only now the club is gaining national and international recognition with celebrities from around the world coming in almost nightly to jam at the Kingston Mines. Albert King, the Allman Brothers, The Rolling Stones, showing up after their own gigs, just to be there.

Doc is a modest man and if you ask him to explain the Mine's success he will stop and pause a moment to think, then point to the logo on the new sign outside which reads, "Chicago Blues Center", or he might talk about the new sound system. Maybe the new sign does make a difference, and perhaps the new sound system helps, but the truth is Doc puts on shows where other clubs will hire a band. Doc might have two, three, sometimes as many as four featured singers, besides a great blues band, perform together on any given night. Even on weeknights before small audiences. If Doc has money he spends it. Doc likes to put together shows. Which is why he drives a 1972 beat-up Ford Torino, while his peer group at the hospital drives Porsches and Mercedes Benz. Doc has his own priorities. Instead of driving a fancy car, Doc owns a nightclub.

Lefty Dizz with Ralph Lappatino Jr. in the background

Saturday Night, July 14, 1979

Eighteen hours and four sets later it is Saturday night, and despite the heat and the broken down cooling systems and the warm beer, the house is packed again with lots of faces familiar from the night before. And Lefty Dizz is no longer shaking, but got his full stride confidence now... and his regular drummer. He made them crazy last night, tonight he was gonna do them in. Wearing his gangster blue pinstripe suit with his diamond lapel stickpin in the shape of his guitar, and his snake shoes dancing, charming that wang-dang-doodle, rolling please, please beat, shattered soul strutting. Dizz singing, "Baby, please don't go/ down to New Orleans/ you know I love you so/ baby, please don't go/ baby, all night long."

Luther Allison sitting in playing Louisiana funeral dirge lead-ins on harp with cold horn backgrounds, incredible haunting chamber crypt riffs. Then changing, (once your chilled skin is pierced), to an up-tempo slurring — gets you right to the bones, "Whisper me sweet nothings, baby/ Whisper me all night long."

Addie gets called up for the second set. Tall slender good looking, hard rocking, sweet street corner blond. "You want to make some love with me, honey?/ Well, come on/ Step right up." Plays guitar like crazy. Crowd really loves her. The way she jumps right in, giving every song she sings, everything she's got. Doing some Willie Dixon tunes, then some Stones, then a tune of her own.

Dizz gets back on stage, after Addie's featured numbers, to close the show. The audience is primed to infinity. Dizz does a few numbers first, walking blues kind of stuff, then swings into a guitar duel *with himself*, playing both sides, competing with that ghost Dizz — Dizz the showman. "I am the baby," he says. "That's right. I am the baby." Dizz talking, making all his funny, half laughing with you faces, and exaggerated supreme gestures. And you know he's right on top of it, you know he's telling you, and somehow it is the way you want to hear it.

Dizz beating that other Dizz sucker cold, telling him at last, "You know now you don't want to come round here trying to compete with me. Not with Lefty Dizz. Cause everybody knows I'm the best there is. Ain't no sense you wanting to mess with me. Shit no. Now just watch this."

Then flings straight on into another wild hard scrapping pick blues jumping miles high just to avoid hitting that other ghost-Dizz-double for one last time, and bone dance boogie, he stops cold like the skin just left the man standing there, naked, chilled, and tough luck stark in the middle of the thunder... lays down his guitar as the band plays on. Dizz, leaving the stage in a slow step, triumphant, victor, taking five from the front row fans. End of set.

Willie Dixon and Addie

Monster Of The Blues Museum

Meanwhile, at the bar, a dramatic scene is unfolding. The participants are three. There is a blond haired, clean cut, suburban biker type, modular chain belt vibes, ugly, big Kawasaki, capped teeth, who looks to be apparently buying drinks for this lovely, good looking, wild eyed blond in a black lace evening gown, pigtails, and not much else. The bar is extremely crowded and people are virtually crawling over each other in order to get close enough to the bartender to order drinks. Lots of raised mixed voices and loud bar rumble in the hot musky room. A scratchy blues record playing on the phonograph. The band is on break time.

The third party in this episode is a lady, as well. She is a bit taller than the other one, not bad looking either, but heavier, and with sandy colored hair. And it is to this second handsome lady that the biker turns his attention, and begins telling her how it has been a month since they first began seeing each other, and how close they are becoming, and how good he feels about it. Really sincere words for a biker. For which the sandy colored girl just stares at him. Then after a few minutes sends him a silent nod of confirmation. She received the message. Two more slow motion seconds go by, then she lays a kiss on his rosy biker cheek.

Meanwhile, the blond in the pigtails and the black lace gown, who seemed to have disappeared for those moments, when her friends were confessing their love, comes back to the bar for a refill. She is drinking tequila sunrises. And while she is hugging and loving up her boyfriend, the biker, who had just paid for her drink, and with her arms still around him, she introduces herself to the bartender, beginning her flirtation with a wink, and developing her friendly "thank you" into a bold proposition to explore all new after hours possibilities, to go where no man has yet ventured to go, (ala Tequila Trek), and that she has had her eyes on him all night, and that she thinks, perhaps, she and him might be able to get a serious friendship going. All of which places a very hostile glare in the eyes of her discarded biker.

The bartender doesn't know what she is talking about. Except he does know exactly what she is talking about, but is simply too busy to listen. Gives her a half cocky, half confused smile, and says, "Sure." Then continues about his business.

The biker, disturbed by the pigtailed lady's outlandish behavior, abandons his conversation with his other girl friend, the larger and silent sandy haired lady, and demands the slender pigtailed beauty give him a kiss. Which she does, enthusiastically.

Then, suddenly, the band is up again on stage and the music begins. The pigtailed lady in the black lace dress grabs her girl friend, the heavier sandy colored woman, and they both go off in the direction of the stage, leaving the clean cut biker alone at the bar. And, as far as I know, the girls never did return.

Lavelle White

Monster, Part II

After closing that night, standing around talking with Doc outside the club, the sun just beginning to come up over the lake, no traffic on the street, no people, just some loose damp sidewalk debris being shuffled along by a wispy silent breeze in the pale thin dawn, a few nickel plated Indiana clouds cutting through an Earl Scheib paint job sky.

It had been some time since I last spoke with Doc and I was interested in getting his views as to what this scene was all about. I was not sure what I was looking for. I wanted to hear some ideas already developed. I wanted to hear an idea or concept already established. . . some *old information* to help support this present.

We were leaning against the front fender of my sky blue Dodge when Doc's daughter came jaunting out the front door of the Mines with the reminder to let Doc know that she had forgotten to have the oil checked in the Ford. Doc told her, "Alright," and said, "Come on," gesturing to me to come with him to check the oil.

We crossed the street to where his car was parked and popped the hood. It was still a bit brisk outside. I picked up a piece of stray newspaper from the curb to wipe the oil stick on, cleaned the oil stick with it, then reinserted the stick back into the block for a measurement, while Doc was checking to see how many quarts of oil he had left from the case he had stored in the trunk of his car. The Ford had a flat-head straight six cylinder engine with a hundred and forty-five thousand miles on it, looked like hell, but still ran like a top: albeit, a pretty worn out top. The oil was alright. The sun was rising higher in the sky now, and it was beginning to get a lot brighter, and the air was turning hot and humid and heavy. We closed the hood of the old Ford and crossed back to the Mines where we used the high window ledge in front of the club to sit on and talk.

I asked Doc what he thought about this scene in comparison to some of the older scenes that had taken place at the Mines, scenes he knew I was familiar with.

"Well, I'll tell you," Doc began, "this is a good lively scene now, and it's gonna get a lot bigger... Real soon, too. You'll see. But in the same respect it has the tendency to get a lot stranger. A lot stranger in some ways. I don't know. It's basically a good scene. But if there is a bad side to the blues scene, it's the women who take the brunt of it. I'm not kidding. Especially the young ones, from the small farm towns in Iowa, or downstate Illinois, who hit the big city, and end up getting fucked around by half a dozen musicians before they know what's happening. And I'll tell you, some of these musicians tear their women up. But there's not much of that going on now.

"I'll tell you something that happened. There was this one musician in particular, who has since been barred from here... He's not allowed to walk into this club anymore... But anyway, he started hanging out at the Mines about a year ago, a guitar player, played with a few different bands, you know, not a bad musician. But, what he'd do. He had this system... When he'd get a young girl interested in him he'd invite her up to a place he had in Canada, some secluded, little place he knew about, for a week or two. Then, once there, the first thing he'd do is beat the shit out of her. I mean, really, just beat her. Something you and I can't even realize happening. But, this is what this guy would do... And then he'd rape the woman a couple of times. Then he'd beat her again. Over and over, beating her up, then raping her, until that woman wouldn't know her name any more.

Lavelle White and Al Simmons

And then he'd tell her. You understand what I'm saying? He'd have that woman so shattered and broken, so personally degraded, terrified, whatever. The woman, at that point, is doing anything he asks. Maybe just to get herself out of there, you know, get the cat to stop beating her. I don't know. I don't know how that works. But the end results are two weeks later they're back in town and she's suddenly working for him in some cathouse. It's true. I saw it happen. Just one time, you can be sure, but that was enough. That will never happen here again. I'll tell you that for certain... Not here. I'd sooner close the room."

It was three or four months later before that particular musician's name was brought up again. Not that his name came up during a conversation, but rather the connection came in the form of a late Sunday night phone call. The caller stated that the body of that musician was found earlier that morning in his car parked somewhere on the far southside. Someone, shot him in the head.

Arrives The Unpress

Robert R. Rudnick, provocateur of menace and self-proclaimed Crown Prince of Sleaze himself, the original all night DJ from Bob's Howling at the Moon Show on Radio Free Detroit, ex-cult columnist for The Rumored-Sun Daily, in NYC, lizard tongue hero of the New Wave, and next to William Burroughs, the only American verse addict answer to Moshe Dayan we've got. And also, a modest friend who earns his living, or more accurately, his life style, by writing a rock gossip column in town, for no particular press. In fact, Rudnick is not published anywhere. He just writes his columns and shows them to people and friends he runs into on his nightly sweeps of media bars, punk joints, and concert halls in the city. Because no newspaper will touch it. Not even the so called counter-culture news sheets. His columns are just that good.

Rudnick called ahead to let us know he was coming, and that he was bringing Commander Cody, who was in town playing the Park West, and who Bob convinced should definitely hit the blues scene for the late night and after hours jam, hot type publicity hype, and that sort of thing. In other words, Bob was bringing over a gang of rowdies, and all he expected in return was his one free beer... Absolutely, Bob. Come on over.

Moments later Bob comes cruising up amidst a stranger than life entourage of human species, consisting of one social economist wearing a Reggie mask, reminiscent to the old Archie Comix Books, who would change his mask for a set of funny

Charlie Watts (Rolling Stones)

glasses and a fake beard and parade around telling everyone he was Zorba the Greek. One depressed tv media man, and nephew to the Dr. Denton baby pajamas fortune, in charge of checks, balances, and miscellaneous gratuities for the night. "Riding book" as they say. One common blind cave dwarf, who wasn't just high on drugs, this guy didn't just take drugs, what this guy would do is first feed the drugs to his dog, then before the dog could shit, he would kill the beast and eat him. The dwarf was relatively mute that night, except for an occasional "oops" everytime he walked into a wall. And lastly, the winner of the 1940's June Allison look-alike contest, playing the part of "The Girl." A splendid group in all. But, as it turned out, Cody never showed up, and old Lizard Tongued Bob, in a frustrated, humiliated, and overwhelming state of inebriated ease, hung out around the bar anyway, accusing ruffians of wearing lace panties, yelling at passers-by for not wearing high enough heeled shoes, while studying the question of shooting up his warming flat beer.

Pretenses Of The Real World

For the past several hours I am listening to a customer tell the bartender about her life, beginning and always coming back to her writing program, at school, and all the facts of life concerning publications, principles of modernisms, how great a playwright she is going to be, because prose is too difficult and poetry gets no respect, her early morning workshop classes, her writing in taverns over beers like F. Scott Fitzgerald and Hemingway, amidst other various bravado, contrary to fact and not, of her life in practiced theory. She likes to speak about herself. The band on stage is a group of Minneapolis imports moving along in slowtime, destined for a one night only. I keep feeling outdoors it is raining, but it isn't. I casually mention to the customer speaking that I am a writer, also. Which she totally ignores, preferring a dialogue of her own concerning how bad a time she is having with men.... because people don't understand writers.

"I see," said the bartender. "But don't you think that is a rather dangerous position to take? I mean, if people don't understand writers, how come they buy the books, and watch so much tv?"

She shakes off his comments for a statement of her own. "I am placing upon my ambitions all the burdens of my social failures," she says. Hasn't had a boyfriend in five years.

"Gee. Too bad," says the bartender.

And, "I am attending graduate school in an attempt to perfect my reasons for catharsis." 23 years old. Short. Overweight. Keeps referring to other women as being flat chested. Can't stop talking. Finally acknowledges the statement I made about being a writer also, and places it in the contents of, "I knew we had something in common."

I tell her I am married and have seven children.

"Oh," she says moving her message back to the bartender.

About 2 a.m. two travellers from New York City come in and the bartender takes the opportunity to play the "Where you from" game, and "How great a town this is welcome." But the talking girl has other plans, and on her own initiative comes around the back bar to where the bartender is standing and interrupts his travelogue conversation with the New Yorker's by suddenly slipping herself beneath the bartender's right shoulder, holding him close with one arm around his waist, his arm responding around her shoulder, her other hand on her hip, standing there as natural as if she had been arm in arm with the bartender a hundred times. And with the bartender's mouth still open, she begins telling the travellers from the east how really great the bartender is to whom they are speaking.

"Hey, wait a minute! What is this?" the bartender says. And there is a tug between her holding on to her hugging position beneath the bartender's shoulder, and him trying to push her away. "What do you think you're doing here?"

"Oh, come on," she tells the bartender. "This is fun."

"Now listen, I don't want you back here," he tells the girl pushing her towards the end of the short service bar to where the entrance and exit is. "Now you just go and sit down before you make me angry."

"What's the matter?" she says resisting all the way. "Are you gay or something?"

"What! What was that?" said the bartender. "What did you say to me?"

"Well, I don't know," she says. "What do I know? Besides, you got those tight jeans on and everything, and there's so many of them in my neighborhood."

"What's the matter with you? What? Are you crazy? What's going on here, anyway?"

"Ok. Ok." she says turning out from behind the back bar towards a stool next to the New Yorkers, and sits down. The bartender, flabbergasted, embarrassed and confused, just stands there glaring at her.

"Well, come on," she says.

"What do you mean, come on? You got a lotta damn nerve."

"Alright. Alright," she tells him and turns away. But there is no more talk or travelogue, that conversation being over. And all that is left in its absence is a silence and an awkwardness.

Some minutes later, interrupting the silence now, she turns back toward the bartender and asks him if he'd like a ride home after work.

"You know something," the bartender begins to tell her, "I think you're a fucking nut case. That's what I think. I think maybe you should go home now. Yeah, that's what I think. You're some kind of looney tunes character, and no thank you. I don't think I want a ride home from you, ok? Thanks anyway."

"Ask me if I have a car?" she says.

"Listen, I think you ought to just get out of here, now!" the bartender tells her.

"No. Just answer me. Do you think I have a car?"

"Listen, I don't think I want to answer you anything."

"Just answer me first and then I'll go."

"What?"

"Come on. Just ask me if you think I have a car?"

"Ok, Do you have a car?"

"No," she replied.

"Listen, I don't think I know what you're trying to do here, but I don't like it," the barman tells her.

"I'm not trying to do a thing, you faggot!" she says.

"Alright! That's it!" he says and comes charging out from around the bar. But the girl beats him to the front door and escapes into the night before he can reach her.

"Can you believe that girl?" the bartender says coming back to his position behind the bar. "Some people you just can't talk to, you know."

"I guess," said one of the New Yorkers.

Carey Bell

Friday Night, July 20, 1979

Carey Bell, the famous southside blues harp player, is headlining the weekend at the Kingston Mines. Ray Moyeno, a young drummer who worked with Carey Bell, worked with Lefty Dizz, worked with a lot of bands before putting together a band of his own, was telling me how rehearsals were held at Carey Bell's house when he was working with his band. No garage band scene there. Rehearsals were held on Sunday afternoons, on the front porch of Carey Bell's southside home. Carey's whole family would be attending. The power in the house would be at times turned off for lack of money to pay the bills, but still on the front porch the band would be jamming. Carey Bell has been singing since he was eight years old. Now his full grown son, Laury Bell, plays lead guitar in his father's band. And on occasion, Carey's younger sons, ages 5, 7, & 9, play in the band, as well.

Laury Bell opens the show with an instrumental number or two, then sings a song himself, before introducing the one and only, Carey Bell. Carey strides up to the stage, takes hold of the microphone and places it beneath his harp, raises the harp to his mouth, bends off a couple test notes. The band immediately cooks. Carey, a big strongly built man, huddled over his harp, dragging the microphone cord behind him, stalking the audience, prowling around the foot of the stage, mingling with the customers like some big wicked host. Finds a tall tequila brown brunette sitting up front who says she wants to dance with him, all night. Carey motioning to her with his eyes, blowing notes at her. The brunette up and dancing before him. Their eyes fixed together. Carey spins around quickly, screams something loud and animal into the microphone, stops and stares at the audience. "Only nineteen years old," Carey Bell is singing.

It is interesting to see that once the music begins to play all the groans of discomfort from the audience stops. The Kingston Mines has unofficially given up hope for repairing the air conditioning system...OUT OF ORDER. And, if anyone asks why it's so hot you simply say, "Because it's summer. That's why." And if anything gets repaired, the leaking roof comes first.

There are three fans set up around the room to keep the smoke moving. Like, "Life before air conditioning."

You can't learn in any school to do what Carey and Laury Bell do. Two full grown men, father and son, a virtual blood-knot lifetime of growth and development together, knowing each other's every move, playing blues harp and lead guitar as if they were just another simple complex form in nature, instead of two. Harmonizing, improvising, fast quick moves. Humming, over and over, drawing you deeper into their rich entangled fabric, magnificent in blues.

Towards the end of the show Lavelle White comes on and does one of her strongest, totally obscene sets she can muster. Hot and tawdry as the summer night air itself, warm and slow, moving those strong, wide, magic hips of hers around, then back to the audience, seducing them. Hypnotizing, something old and earthly kingdom. You can actually feel her body move, like the sound of a bass chord, all the way in the back of the room. Driving people in the audience crazy.

"Yes, I'm just crazy," she told me later.

Steve Cropper, Carey Bell, Albert Collins, Donald "Duck" Dunn, Dan Aykroyd and John Belushi

*Albert Collins, Steve Cropper, Ray Moyeno, Donald "Duck" Dunn,
Dan Aykroyd, Billy Branch and John Belushi*

Tell Me, Why Do Young Men Go Wild

Keeping a low profile in the back of the room, watching Carey Bell and the band work, was John Belushi and Dan Aykroyd, the two guys from the network hit tv show, *Saturday Night Live*, who were touring the country with an act based on their popular skit called The Blues Brothers. They had an album out that was surprisingly good, and were in Chicago filming a full length feature film based on their Blues Brothers act.

Belushi had been in and out of the club several times during the past couple of weeks, and it was nice to see "the home town boy made good" back in town. But tonight he had his partner, Dan Aykroyd, with him, and a small party besides. Nevertheless, keeping pretty anonymous throughout the first couple of sets. Till about midnight when John Belushi decided to let his presence be known.

I should say, first off, that John Belushi is the only person I have ever met who is more recognizable with dark glasses on, rather than off. But it would be easy to say that Belushi allowed people to recognize himself by just putting his dark glasses on. The dark glasses are a necessary prop, granted. And, true, we only know this man by the faces he broadcasts to us over the media. But what was fascinating to see was the changes he made in his face to make himself look more like his tv self, or for that matter, how he spent the first part of the evening enjoying himself as just another face in the crowd by simply *not* looking like himself. When he didn't want to attract attention he was pale faced and timid in appearance. And now he was suddenly full of color and bold, dark shades on and aggressive. Dan Aykroyd, on the other hand, looked like any common gasoline attendant in the midwest, and stayed that way.

Doc showed up about that time, and gave Belushi and Aykroyd the full welcome treatment; couple rounds of drinks in the VIP Room, and got the scoop on the movie and so forth. Then introduced these Blues Brothers to some of the band members and musicians in the house; Carey Bell, Albert Collins, Aron Burton. Then out of custom and courtesy, Carey Bell invited Dan Aykroyd and John Belushi to sit in and do a couple numbers of their own, next set, if they wanted to. Which they did. And a giant jam session became immediately planned. Everyone was gonna get in on it. Lavelle White was gonna start the set off, and then Carey Bell would announce his guests in order.

There was a great excitement building up in the room. Then the music began. The first thing Lavelle White did when she got on stage was to blow the roof right off its rafters. Took the damn roof right off. There's not a woman in Chicago who can sing with the power and authority of Lavelle White, and she gave a good example of what power and authority was, starting off her set with a song of her own, *Tell Me, Why Do Young Men Go Wild,* and ending her set with that song as well, stacking the middle with *Red Rooster* and *Bright Lights, Big Titties, Have Gone To My Baby's Head.* A blockbuster medley to set up these blockbuster guests. Then Carey Bell introduced his other guests; Albert Collins, the Ice Picker, and Master of the Stratocaster, himself; Aron Burton, the bassman's bassman in Chicago; Jimmy Johnson, who can't walk on water, but has been seen skating on gasoline; Laury Bell, the backup group, and these two tv heroes, The Blues Brothers.

When Carey introduced The Blues Brothers the whole audience went wild giving them a standing ovation. Truly these two men were living idols of the little screen. People actually stay home on Saturday nights just to watch them on tv. And here they are, in person. What a surprise, Friday Night Live at The Kingston Mines. And the audience was standing up and letting their appreciation show. This was as exciting as the night The Rolling Stones showed up. Maybe even more.

The ovation went on for ten or fifteen minutes, with Aykroyd and Belushi making small attempts throughout that time to try to settle the audience down. Really hamming it up though. Belushi doing animal imitations on stage. King Kong radio hour. Roars, and Frankenstein stalking moves. Appeasing the audience with his silliness. Meanwhile, the band is standing around making the best of it, wondering what "you Blues Brothers want to play?" "I don't know?" "Pick a standard." "Ok. Sweet Home Chicago." "Fine."

When the audience finally settled down, the band jumped into the number. But the band got short circuited somehow. It wasn't noticeable at first, because this was a jam, and the band was so strong. But what happened was that Belushi and Aykroyd kept failing to pick up their leads. You know, like, "Take it, boys." And the boys don't take it. Not that the audience cared at all. They were satisfied just seeing these guys on stage and getting that extra tale to tell their friends at work on Monday morning.

The audience was having no problem at all watching this all-star band carry Aykroyd and Belushi. After all, these Blues Brothers were actors first, and musicians second. Nor do I think it bothered Dan Aykroyd. Aykroyd finally getting through a set of lyrics simple enough, then just stood around, half dancing, half hanging out on stage, cruisin' along with the show. But John Belushi kept getting caught with that harp in his mouth and refusing to blow.

Well, so what, you can say. So what, indeed! This man is one of the great comic actors of our time, and if he can't suddenly become the great blues musician over night, well, we can deal with that. I mean, who cares anyway ?

John Belushi cared. And after the first number he ran off stage and fought his way through the roaring, cheering support of the crowd to the bar and ordered a shot, "Quick, of Courvoisier," downed it, then said to the bartender, "I got to get out of here!"

The bartender didn't know what he was talking about, but poured him the shot and said, "Uh, huh."

Meanwhile, the whole room was calling for more. To which Belushi replied, "Forget it!"

Fans followed him to the bar calling for songs off their album, saying, "Come on, man. Let's hear some blues!"

"No way," was Belushi's reply.

The crowd kept coming at him, and for their support he told them to, "Forget it! Go home!"

"Go home?" The crowd couldn't understand it. How absurd to be told to "Go home."

Then Belushi, himself, ran out the front door.

The band couldn't understand it, either. Carey Bell asked over the p.a. system to "Come on, man. Let's get some jams going here."

Nothing doing. The room was in total confusion. Everyone calling for, "More! More!"

Then a few minutes later Belushi came back into the room to verify the fact that he wasn't going to do any more. It was something the audience did not want to hear.

The friendly support of the crowd became ugly. "What do you mean, go home?"

People began grabbing Belushi in the aisle and pelting him with insults. But he fought his way through the mob screaming statements like, "Leave me alone! No, I'm not going on! That's it! Too bad! Forget it! Go home!" Then ran out the front door of the club for good.

No one was sure what was going on. Aykroyd was still up front on stage. But the set was totally disrupted. Carey Bell, in an attempt of courtesy, to himself, as well as the audience, promised Belushi would be back for more songs. But the crowd wouldn't settle down. And after a while, Carey Bell, too, realized Belushi was not returning to the stage, felt the insult, and said to hell with him. "Fuck those guys," he told the audience. "I've been on tv, too, goddamnit. Blues Brothers... shit. All us people are the real blues brothers... That's right. So let's get on with the show." Which they did.

Big Walter Horton

The Intimacy of Telepathy

And it's way later now, near the end of Carey Bell's last set, nearly 5 a.m., all the smoke cleared away and only a small intimate audience left in the club, when Lefty Dizz walks in. It feels like days have gone by, the long night past full of surprises hangs in the air. Then Lefty Dizz enters the club and Carey Bell immediately calls Lefty up to the stage. Or maybe Dizz just gets up there himself. Who knows, the intimacy of the room at this point is so high it might as well be telepathy.

"Let's let Lefty Dizz have some," Carey Bell chimed over the brain waves. "Yeah, let's let Lefty Dizz have some." And Lefty turns towards the voice calling him up, never breaking stride since walking through the door. Dizz could have been walking through water the way he handled the room, his feet leading the way, his tall lean body catching up. He could have been cutting across a field of tall grasses, a mild wind painting the soft vegetation, the room luscious and full.

Last call.

Dizz not even using a microphone. Voice raspy and wild. Dizz standing at the foot of the stage, pacing back and forth in front of the band, jumping in and out from one aisle to another, singing his verses. The whole audience calling back to him in response. Dizz, making up his lyrics as he goes along, no melody line, just rhythm and words, and the audience clapping and shouting back to him.

You don't have to worry,
I'll be your slave,
I'll work for you, baby,
Till I'm in my grave.

Now, ain't that nice...
To be in love that way.

Ain't that nice, ain't that nice, ain't that nice...
To be in love with you.

Lavelle White, Johnny Dollar in background

Not Fade Away

The next night, at 2 a.m., the club is raided by police who were informed by someone over the telephone that minors were drinking at the Kingston Mines. All of which was untrue....to a point. Which means there were minors drinking at the bar. Laury Bell, for instance, is only 20 years old. The legal drinking age in Illinois is 21. Also, a couple of the girls working the floor as bussers and runners for the regular help, are minors. But they were working, not drinking, and were quickly hustled out the back door while the police made spot checks through the audience in search of a young one. They didn't find any. But what they did find, when inspecting the club's operating licences on the wall, was that one of the licences was missing. The missing paper was the late night licence making it legal to sell alcohol until 4 a.m. nightly, and 5 a.m. on Saturdays. The late night licence previously hanging on the wall with the other licences was gone. So Doc and Mary were forced to clear the room and close up two hours early.

The Inside Track

Everything is associated with the club. You go there to work. Hang out. Feel good. Ladies and gentlemen, you shall experience a total sensory distortion the moment you walk through the doors. Your sense of smell will be neutralized upon contact with the heavy wash of cigarette smoke. Vision is filtered through the humidity characteristic of summer, and jarred by the presence of being in a room with several hundred people, the dark lights and orange walls, the wafts of grey smokey clouds drifting slowly as a vapor excited by waves of sound rushing through its porous brilliancy, and people on the move within this unique atmosphere. The audio is simply deafening. Layers of highly ordered and amplified sound, coupled with a rich fabric of people's voices, yelling, and laughing. All this mixing together for something ultimately pleasant. A certain level of excitement. A limited world within its own. There is no food to eat, only liquor to drink. Conversations are short, and more times than not half the words spoken are lost in the loud music, so what you get is alot of edited dialogue, which is usually something else. Your normal tone of voice is shouting. You get your sleeping done during the day. You'll get to know that special quietness of the world experienced only at daybreak, while walking through the park, or along the lakefront after a night spent at the club. A beer or two in hand, a couple of joggers in the distance. That special effect of sunrise after a long night's work. When all the birds are in the air swirling around in grand formations, celebrating their morning exercise. When all the trees seem to sparkle with the reflection of that rising break of orange sun. The world is quiet and marvelous. Like you've never known it before.

Willie Dixon and The Chicago All-Stars

La La La La La Bom-ba

Now just because you are a competent musician and you know the chords don't mean you can play blues, because blues is not just a music but a form of emotional expression, and if you don't know what it is to give it everything you've got, (and there is room for the laid back, but not the emotionally laid back) and keep it tight as well – because I've seen guys get up there and try it, with all the imitation word phrasing and gestures – don't make it. It can't be done that way.

And I'm not speaking as if this were any one particular problem. All cliches aside, the blues has a "tonal quality" attached with being able to succeed personally with it, rather than fail at a simple statement you would think is necessary for any blues performer to make. For instance, how you feel. You can't fake it. There is no room for faking it. Because blues strives for a tone of quality. Of originality. Of honesty. You have to be your own man up there. This is America. We are the United States. And if you can't hit that tone to begin with, your shows will be dull and your career with be short.

Willie Dixon and Billy Branch

The Buddha Of Blues

The newspaper reads, "There will be no head transplants performed in South Africa." News of which is a relief for many of us to hear, certainly. The conviction is that a head transplant (performed successfully, so far, on only rabbits and dogs), would be immoral, and besides, present technology does not permit the spinal column of the body to be connected to the patient's head properly, so as to allow the arms and legs of the recipient's new body to work, so "what's the sense?" sayeth the newspaper. I don't know. I think they should wake up Walt Disney from his deep freeze sleep and ask him.

Finish my morning coffee, put the newspaper down and go to work. Go to my job. Gather and evaluate the data, then write the story. I am involved in a limited anthropology; the anthropology of contemporary Chicago urban blues.

In a sense the Mines is always the same. Premise — live music every night. Experimenting with new shows for audience response occurs on weeknights. You build your acts on weeknights for the big weekend crowds. Plus you want to have that extra big draw idea or two for holiday nights or an occasional Sunday afternoon. And yet, no two nights at the Mines are ever the same. Each night is more a study in combinations. Bands are always shifting personnel. People are always showing up on any night to jam. And shows are often influenced by the audience response, as well as a thousand other factors: i.e., if the van carrying the equipment blows a tire on the expressway, the show starts late.

Watching a tv interview, recently, I enjoyed what the playwright, Arthur Miller, had to say of most live theater in America today. He said, "It is in error to say to your wife, 'Hey, honey, let's go see a play tonight,' because what you should be saying is, 'Hey, honey, let's go see some business tonight,' because what you're getting today, for the most part, is not a play at all, but is, in fact, business. You know, like where's the play? The point is...the term 'play' means more than just going to a job, which happens to be playing a role in a theatrical production. The term 'play' means, and always has meant, getting yourself up there on stage and enjoying yourself in the process of your performance."

There are factors to be considered. And rehearsals in the blues world are rare. Yet, a good blues performance is no less theatrical, and as much a part of the "play" as Arthur Miller has suggested. When Lefty Dizz is performing, every turn of his wrist, every wink of his eye, every movement, in fact, that he makes is developed over a series of years. And is as much a part of his song as lyrics, chord progression, or his rhythm section. Everything he does on stage is part of his music. When you hear Jimmy Johnson sing, "I've got the Saint Louis blues, as blue as I can get/ I sent Louis to the liquor store, and he hasn't come back yet," you know he is entertaining you. He is up there for that purpose.

Take for example, having Willie Dixon in the audience. And it is always a great night when you have Willie Dixon in the audience. The Buddha Of Chicago Blues, himself. The way it takes him twelve or twenty bars just to get him on his feet. Big man with the rolling smile. Then you watch him move. About half way to the bandstand he has his right hand suddenly up close to his chest, his fingers snapping, as if he couldn't stop his fingers from snapping if he wanted to. Not one movement in his body wasted. As if the man's whole existence was designed just to sing the blues. All the perfect rhythms drumming through his limbs. Head back belting out those crocodile tones. Willie Dixon standing clearly a full head taller than anyone in the room. Like he's the singer in the tower. Up there doing it, and taking it all the way. Taking the whole audience with him. No stopping Willie Dixon once you get him started.

End Of The Day Revisited

Lock the doors. Go down the street to the taco joint for a late night dinner. Or take a beer to the lake and watch the sun come up. The disadvantage of being the late night music blues bar is that after closing there is no later bar to go to relax, have a drink, catch the last set jams. Though you can go home. Work is over. Kiss the wife and have your dinner. Walk the dog. Water the lawn. Paint the apartment. Build a garage. Do just about anything. Just as long as you make sure you sleep eventually, because tomorrow night this is all going to happen once again.

Willie Dixon at Chicagofest

The Attack

Blues is the most influential single form of modern music in the western world today. No longer is blues the minority folk medium it was just thirty or forty years ago. Jazz greats and rock n' roll has changed all that allowing bigger audiences to enjoy the music that is, by and large, not too unfamiliar to them anyway. I mean "Elroy James got nothing on me," is a line right off a Beatle's album produced over ten years ago. Blues is very hip. But this Chicago urban blues... They got a drum beat called "The Attack." People come to Chicago from all parts of the world, just to get a dose. For instance, Lionel Hampton showing up one night to jam. This kind of news gets around.

Willie Dixon Speaking with Foghat

You Can Look At It This Way

You can look at it this way,
The blues has it's roots in Mississippi.
That's where it began.
Highway 61 is the stem,
Which leads you to Chicago,
Which, for the blues, is the flower,
The actual rose.

"Big Bad" LeRoy Brown

Scenario No. 23

Blues Fan:	Hey man, you were really great. I mean that last set was dynamite.
Blues Star:	Thank you.
Blues Fan:	I mean you were really good. I don't know. What can I say?
Blues Star:	I don't know.
Blues Fan:	Let me buy you a drink.
Blues Star:	Sure. Ok.
Blues Fan:	What are you drinking?
Blues Star:	Crown Royal and coke.
Blues Fan:	I'll have one too.
Blues Star:	Here's to you.
Blues Fan:	Thanks.

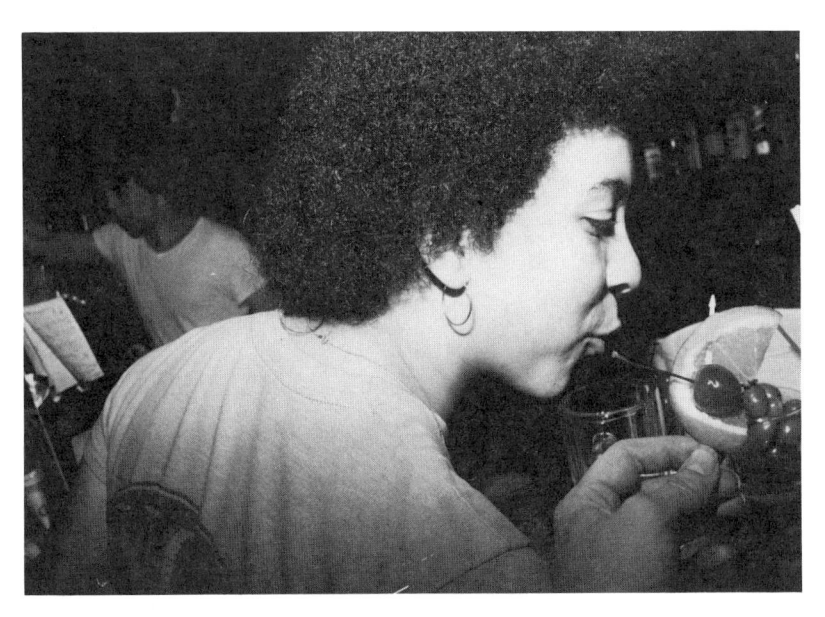

Crew Members

Albert King and Addie

Hounds In The Evening, *(bitches in the night)*

The Mines is now a 2 o'clock bar. Considering the Mines is only open for business a brief seven hours per night, cutting that seven hour period down to five, on a business level, is quite devastating. City Hall would not issue a duplicate late night liquor licence. "No two-for-one sale here." You are not suppose to misplace your operating permit. But what smells like a pig farm in the height of a Nebraska summer is the fact that only employees, and ex-employees of the Kingston Mines, are aware that several of Doc's workers are under age. Yet, when the cops arrived that night they asked specifically, by name, for one of those employees. Fortunately, that particular under age waitress, sought by the cops, had a set of fake I.D.'s stating she was, in fact, quite legal. Yet, the ugly truth remains that someone had called the authorities and reported this waitress as being a minor employed by the Mines in violation of the law. The question is who did the reporting, and even more dastardly, who stole the liquor license off the back bar wall?

A motive for malice and intent. The story behind the event goes something like this: the head bartender for the past couple of years was fired just the week before. Her name was Jan Bramwell. Jan had been employed at the Mines on and off, for over two years, and had been, at one time, manager of the Kingston Mines. But, that was before Mary Hobbs came along. Also, it should be noted that Mary Hobbs and Jan Bramwell had been very close friends back then. Hardly the case of late. Nevertheless, when Mary arrived on the set, her and Doc got together, and that led to the stable and present seat of authority. While, at the same time, Jan's relationship with Mary, and her other fellow employees, began to strain, to the point where prior to her dismissal, Jan was getting along with no one. Her and Mary were not on speaking terms. And it was considered well known that Jan was on her way out.

Also, involved in this scenario is a third party. A lady by the name of Chrisy Lanier. Chrisy had been fired some time ago, but is still remembered for being diabolical and extraordinarily attractive. She was the one who organized a waitress strike on a Saturday night protesting against Doc for not promising the girls a guarantee against tips for an up coming Sunday afternoon event. That strike led to her dismissal. And ever since her memory has grown to legendary proportions. For instance, she was the master thief of waitressing. The one who could double her income on any night of the week despite who was working behind the bar pouring her drinks and collecting her receipts. How she achieved this feat was never explained to me and remains a mystery. She was the ingenious and clever one. The beautiful and persuasive one. The lady who manipulated everyone. Who also happened to be Jan Bramwell's lover. And who supposedly was the brains and motivating force behind this entire incident. The one who was wicked enough to use Jan Bramwell as her emissary of revenge and ill will.

I have my reservations, all this being strictly circumstantial, if not indeed mythological. However, it was only some days earlier, before the bust, that I was visited by Jan Bramwell while I was sitting at the bar. I offered to buy her a drink, but she declined my offer. She instead asked me for my phone number. "Just in case something weird happens," is the way she put it.

"Something weird?" I replied.

"Yes," she told me.

I gave it to her. I didn't understand the problems she was having at the Mines, and didn't involve myself to find out. I personally liked Jan Bramwell, and appreciated her efficiency behind the bar, and in fact practiced a somewhat casual friendship with her. She was cynical, but I liked cynics. However, I later wondered why I would give out my phone number to someone who promised to call in case of weirdness. Did I want to be phoned up and told something weird? Was this expected of one involved in a customer (ex-employee)/bartender over the counter casual relationship? I supposed I found the intrigue of her candid offer too fascinating to pass up. She never did call. And I have not seen her since. Yet, if the ruse of this affair be placed on her, I suspect the peeling of the license from off the wall behind the bar came sometime around the time of this, her friendly warning.

Of course, a story like this would hardly hold up in court, nor will it ever get to court. The important thing is that despite who the culprit may be, the fact remains that Doc has lost two very real hours of business per night, and consequently a substantial loss in receipts. And all of this just in time for the arrival of the summer rains, and the necessity to repair the very large and leaking Kingston Mines roof.

Eddie "The Chief" Clearwater

The Show Goes On

There is a music festival, began at noon, outdoors on Lincoln Avenue. Three stages going simultaneously. Rock, folk, blues, jazz, punk...even a puppet show. Eddie Clearwater did three sets out on the street and another three sets that night at the Kingston Mines, each set better than the last. From the fifties era on, doing a whole review of rockabilly Johnny B. Goode, that Chuck Berry synthesis. Amazing energy. Eddie Clearwater clearly supplies the link between the blues tradition and rock. As a matter of fact, Eddie Clearwater might very well be Johnny B. Goode, before he steps right back into some long distance guitar humming, tight band, hard blues rocker.

But then you walk down the street and there, suddenly, hipped out and shinning in the afternoon sun is another band pumping out what it's all about, a fast talking group called B. B. Spin, taking that same hard ground Chicago energy to the full side rock. "For me/there will always be/an underground." No mistake about it, and I'm just reporting here, just being here at this moment, but one has to occasionally stop and wonder why this town doesn't, in fact, dominate the entire music industry. Too cold, lousy weather, and not enough women laying naked around the available L.A. swimming pool is the answer that keeps popping up.

Margo Smith and Al Simmons

Strictly Southside

After hours Friday night and I'm suppose to meet three waitress friends, Barbara Daniel, Margo Smith, and Sally Sohn, for breakfast down the street at Campeche's all night taco joint. But I never make it. The band and their entourage of wives, children, mistresses, and friends won't leave, and it's Doc's party, and I get caught up in the flow. And by the time I get out, its too late. Campeche's has been left in a shambles.

This is what happened at Campeche's. Several of the restaurant's regulars approached my lady friends with a line or two, which is alright. They're good looking girls who work in a honky-tonk and get approached with lines all the time. And they know how to deal with lines as well. The girls simply declined the offer. But the locals, I gathered, couldn't sit still with the rejection and began laying insults at the ladies, which proved to be to their misfortune, because what happened next could probably be credited to the deviate actions of three no bullshit too high to fuck with ladies, just off work and in no mood for, but instead was orchestrated, in fact, by one lone, and sassy, faster than lightning good looking blond from the southside, Margo Smith, head waitress at the Mines, who aided with a devilish grin, and with the greatest of circus ease, cut her antagonist off with a simple, "Oh yeah, sucker," reaching for the closest object at hand, which happened to be a water glass filled with municipal tap, and heaved the entire contents over her shoulder at her unsuspecting suitor. Though Margo didn't just heave the water, but let go of the glass as well. And then the next glass, and then the next, and then the plates filled with leftover quesadilla and beans, the forks and spoons, and then the napkin container, and even her chair, all in about twenty seconds.

Margo Smith wrecking Campeche's.

The guys made for a quick exit with Margo, Sally and Barbara hot in pursuit. The flight turning into a mad car chase.

Now, you have to know Margo and how she drives to appreciate the story. Margo knows no bounds when it comes to driving. Occasionally she might stop for a red light, if she's not in a hurry, drives on either side of the street, and is generally famous for turning a trip to the supermarket into a gran prix experience. Streets become toboggan trails. Her car becomes a skateboard. Wheels screeching the asphalt in the middle of the night. Margo, gunning her beat up Toyota.

Margo was gaining on her assailants, not quite sure what she would do if she caught them, but gaining nevertheless, when the guys hooked a right onto the freeway entrance ramp. And Margo, going too fast to make the turn, missed the ramp and flew the curb ending up on a soft green hill, shaken, but totally alive, the ladies half in hysterics laughing.

Dimestore Fred

Dimestore Fred, Doc's day porter, at the Mines. Two degrees in math. Gave up a lucrative position with a big bank in Cleveland, his home town, for music. Resident rockabilly blues harp player. Likes the concept of a drunken brawl. Spends his sleeping hours in some weird, transient hotel off Sheffield and Belmont Avenue called Jack's Tokyo Spa. A natural showman. Fred is always giving you the impression he is enjoying his act as much as you are. Wears a three piece double knit black linen zoot suit. Hair slicked back to duck tailed 50's hipster. Has lunch everyday at Beefy LaMeat's. Sells harp lessons on the side. Tours with the Eddie Clearwater Band. Drinks lots of beer. Probably the most outrageous character on the entire blues circuit. Clowning all the time. Getting people to chase after him. Threats to his life a common occurrence. Studied harp with Big Walter Horton. Used to play with Lee Jackson at the B.L.U.E.S. on Halsted Street, Wednesday nights before Lee Jackson passed away.

"How did he die?"

"His wife shot him," said Fred. "Shot him dead. Shot him right through the back of the head."

"Bad taste in women."

"Yeah, that's right," said Fred.

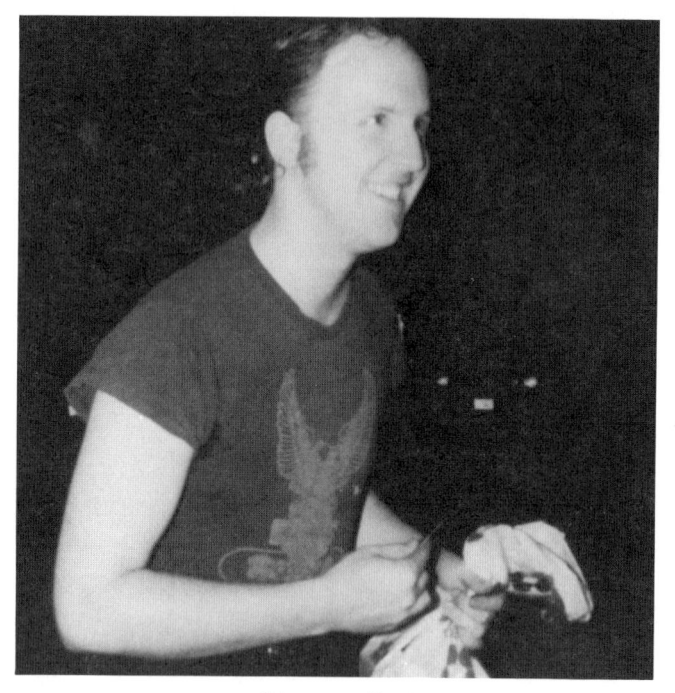

Dimestore Fred

Blind Jim Brewer

Walking past the No Exit Cafe the other night, the landmark coffee house on the far northside of the city, I stopped in and heard a story by the grand old master himself, Blind Jim Brewer, sitting up there at the front of the room by the microphone, just him and his guitar, talking and singing the blues. The story I heard him tell was about a man whose life had taken a turn for the worse. The man and his wife had separated but they were trying to work it out. Because they still loved each other and were hoping to get back together.

"On the good days she wants to have my child.
On the bad days she talks about the money."

But the man felt good about the progress they were making and was confident things were going to work out.

Then a friend came by from out of town.

"Good to see you again, and all that stuff."

But this friend guesses right away that the man and his wife have separated and asks the man for his wife's phone number. This friend coming to visit, standing in the man's living room admiring his wife's photograph on the wall. Staring at it. The man questions his friend's motives for being so interested in his wife, why he keeps asking him questions about his wife. He gets angry at last thinking his friend must be an idiot or something, or maybe his friend thinks he's an idiot. The visiting friend fumbles indignation, eventually finds his way to the door and leaves.

The man tells his wife the story that night and they both laugh about it. She teases him with it, using the experience to their own advantage. Then two days later the man runs into his wife on the street and she is strange to him, distant, and something is obviously wrong. He can feel it. Something is obviously wrong.

The next morning he calls her up and she is irritable and nasty tempered. But they had plans to have a picnic that day, and friends were invited. He tells his wife if she doesn't want to go she doesn't have to, but she says she will. She wants to go. And then he knows just what's the matter. And he tells her, and she says that's right. She was out last night with another man. Not his friend from out of town, but just another man. But that makes no difference to him who she was out with. It is just that she was out. And now he feels so bad, like all the good they had been working on and doing to get back together again is gone, as if the bridge they had been building together just fell apart in the water. And now he feels betrayed and lonely.

But the man still loves his wife. He loves her. And though he knows in his heart, frozen up with the pain, that they'll never get back together now, that things will never again be the same, that he's got to lose, he's got to cut her free to be free, he's stuck there feeling like a love sick fool, because he can't believe what she did to him. For no reason he can think of. But he can't keep playing the fool for her, and now he's got to set her free.

*"If you see me coming down the street, baby,
don't you even look my way.*

*If you see me on the street, woman,
you better walk the other way,*

*Cause you hurt me now, you know that, woman,
and you'll be sorry about it some day."*

Matt Murphy and Sunnyland Slim

Johnny Dollar

Johnny Dollar

Been shot five times. Once in the wrist, three times across various body trunk locations, once in the head. Plays what is known as a "Cold Guitar." Has a smile that immediately charms you. Fought four years in the Marine Corps. Viet-Nam. Twelve years on the Chicago Police Force. Drives a Fleetwood Cadillac with two sun-roofs. Six foot five inch Sagitarian little brother to blues great, Lefty Dizz...who calls his younger brother, Johnny Dollar, "The Outlaw." Plays Sunday nights at the Kingston Mines.

Johnny Dollar walks in, black linen suit, black short brim felt baretta hat. There is a message that his drummer fell sick. Or the drummer's car fell sick. Or his cab fell sick. That he is stranded on 131st Street on the far southside and was not coming in. "That man's a problem to me," says Johnny, then makes the phone call to secure another drummer. It is early evening, about 8:30 p.m., thirty minutes before the club opens. There is no one at the bar except myself, the bartender, a waitress, her boyfriend, and Johnny Dollar. Besides looking vaguely alike, what homespun characteristics Lefty and Johnny share is their gift for incessant story telling.

"It was during the first Jr. Wells tour of Europe," Johnny Dollar speaking, "and he took all of us guys with him; me, Lefty, Jimmy Johnson, Buddy Guy, all of us. I remember Jimmy Johnson was having a hard time with the summer heat, always taking off his shirt and sweating, moaning about it, especially down around Algiers when we were always cramming onto those buses getting from place to place with those people and their crazy chickens and everything else they bring with them. You know the stories. But I'm too hyper, you know, to let the heat bother me. I just kept talkin' and drinking that North African rum, talkin' shit and having a good time. Heat didn't bother me.

"But, what was I saying? Oh yeah, we were swimming off the coast of Algiers. And you know how the beaches are in Algiers? They're real pretty and clean and very shallow. You know, you can walk straight out into the ocean for miles. The water never gets any deeper than maybe chest high. So that's what we're doing. Walking out there for miles. Can't even see the people on the beaches no more. We're just talkin' and swimming and having a good time out there pushing before us this gallon jug of rum, wrapped in one of those wicker basket weavings, right. You know what I'm talking about. Then suddenly I just can't do it no more. And the water's no longer so shallow. I mean we've been swimming for awhile at this point, instead of just walking, not even thinking about it, let alone worrying about it, and I just tired out.

"So, no more sandy reefs waist high water, right. Big surprise. So I'm out there in the Atlantic Ocean with my brother and these other cats, and I'm going down, right. I'm letting myself drift down to the bottom thinking the water is still shallow, with the idea that I'm gonna rest up in the process, and when I reach bottom I'm gonna just spring back up with my legs. Except there is no bottom. And rather than stick around and wonder where the bottom is I start swimming back up thinking, uh huh, I don't think I want to drown here, right. Also, realizing this is for real. You know, deep water for real. But this is where, I'll tell you...now Dizz and I, we fight like brothers, and carry on and all, but you know deep down inside we really love each other."

All of us sitting around now wondering how Lefty Dizz rescued his brother. But that's not exactly the way it happened.

"Let me tell you," says Johnny. "So I'm swimming up trying to get back to the surface, and when I finally get there, before I even take that first breath of air, my brother's yelling, 'You big dummy! Johnny Dollar! You come all the way here, all the way to Europe just to drown! Goddamit, Johnny Dollar, is that what you're gonna do? You big dummy!' And that kind of stuff."

The bartender leans over the bar now wondering what happened. How Dizz managed to save John, and how they both eventually got back to shore.

"Well, I'll tell you," said Johnny. "There were some other guys closer to us who actually held me up, but how my brother saved me was by yelling at me. Because what he did by yelling at me was he made me mad, you see? To the point where I got stronger just by being angry at my brother for yelling that stuff. Then these guys came by in a boat, finally, and picked us up.

"But, I'll tell you, you want to know what the first thing I said was when they got me into that boat?"

"Sure, what?" was our chorus of responses.

"Gimme another shot of that rum," said Dollar.

And we all decided to have one.

Later that night, after closing…and it had been a good night, with Jimmy Johnson doing a great guest number on electric organ. Jimmy said he usually doesn't play the organ, though he knows how, but as long as one's there, he sat down and did a great jazzy blues version of *House Of The Rising Sun*. And Aron Burton did a song. And a two lady vocal group, named Fantasy, actually mimed a song on stage while their 45 rpm record aired across the room on a rear speaker attached to the house stereo. Like some kind of Soul Train thing. Johnny even interviewed the group's manager on stage, in a cloak of seriousness, while the audience tittered, "Yeah, right."

And Lefty Dizz came by and helped his brother close out the final set, going through their "who taught who what" routine, and "who's actually whose big brother." Leading Dollar into a second story after the show was over and the house was cleared out, having an after hours drink at the bar. The story took place one night last winter.

"It was just after New Year's Eve. Remember the snow was about this high," Johnny said showing with his hand how the snow had accumulated about waist high. "Dizz was playing that night, and I'm just hanging out by the front door when this car pulls up carrying four guys and a girl. I mean four big guys, and they all got guns. So the chick jumps out of the car and she's carrying a .45 in each hand, and comes up to me at the door. And I say, 'What are you doing?' And she says, 'I've come to shoot Lefty Dizz.' And I say, 'You've come to shoot Lefty Dizz?' And she says, 'That's right. I've come to kill him.'

"Now, I don't know this girl from nothing. Never seen her before. But I tell you, I don't mess around with talk like that...especially when the talk's carrying a gun. Because I know about that stuff. Because I told you I've been shot before. So I just take those guns away from that girl and rap her once with one on the side of her ear, then turn her around and put those two gun barrels to the back of her head...just like that."

Johnny showing us how he did it using his index fingers for gun barrels.

"And marched that lady right back to her car and told those guys in the car to throw out their guns. I want them all, I told them, right there in the snow. And they threw them all right there, too. Then I told the girl to get back in the car and for them to drive away. Which they did. Then I took those guns and threw them all on top of that two flat building down the street. Except for the two .45's...I kept them, and still got them at home to this day."

"That's right," said Dizz. "That outlaw brother of mine, Johnny Dollar, comes walking back in here with them two .45's strapped to his sides, pleased as he can be. I never even knew what was going on. People came up and told me about it later. That's right. You think I got something to worry about with that outlaw brother of mine around? No way, I tell ya. Taught him everything he knows, too."

Detroit Jr. and Friends

Armed To The Teeth

The serious aspects of the blues as an original American music can be viewed in terms of its development from slave days to contemporary urban electronics. But this, of course, has been researched by many a student of blues far better than I have any wish or inclination to do. It has been done. And if the musicians, today, are not interested in this, ("Hey Lefty, what about the new blues?" "What new blues?," says Lefty Dizz), then why should I be?

What interests me is being here, at this place in time, at this club with these people, and recording the events that occur. But what I occasionally fall into is the industry shop talk. Like speaking with Richard Harding, the owner of the Quiet Knight, the great old night spot on the northside, now closed. Harding knows the business well. Knows how the record companies make their money. Knows how the musicians, even the successful ones, sometimes end up making no money at all. Harding deals directly with the record companies for his bookings, and is thinking about reopening his club and going punk...an indicator to the future.

But back to what interests me is how blues, the roots and basis for all these other contemporary musical forms, has never taken off on the charts or established itself as an independent movement in the music industry. Though there has always been, and most likely always will be, some hot mainstream pop star cruiser covering the blues; i. e., Jimi Hendrix, Joe Cocker, Joni Mitchell, or Simply Red. Maybe it is because the blues is not a new thing, but very old. Whereas punk, for instance, is new. And probably blues will always be a springboard for new commercial movements to draw a fresh idea from.

Shop talk has it how the music industry would not even touch punk until their indicators were certain they could produce a star that would guarantee at least 12 million sales per album. But blues survives. Because blues is cult and contemporary at the same time. Open for adventure and discovery, and is yet familiar. Blues supplies the space for musical heroics. Who is that giant black man in the lime green suit with the rocket ship guitar strapped over his shoulder? Who are these strange cats dressed in wild bright colors creating their own personal stage filled with chants and shouting diatribes which seem to relate to our lives, armed to the teeth with their mystic calls and screams, and shiny electronic instruments, blasting audio allusions and images to the world? Who are these guys, anyway? Where do they come from? And how do they survive?

These Guys Don't Care

These guys don't care if you want to jam with a trumpet, or a saxophone, or a pot belly stove. If you have the chops, if you can hit the lick, you can sit in. As simple as that. No academics or purists here. This is space, man. These people are into their music. Making music is what is happening this evening.

Detroit Junior

Speaking With Lefty Dizz

AS: Lefty, how'd you go from an Air Force fighter pilot to a blues musician?

LD: You want to know how I got to be a blues musician? Well, I'll tell you how.

AS: Yeah, tell me.

LD: Alright, I'm gonna tell you.

AS: And I want to know what happened to the Carthaginians, also.

Lefty Dizz

Doc and Lefty Dizz

LD: The Carthaginians! I know about them goddamn Carthaginians. I went to college you know. I'm a goddamn college graduate. Southern Illinois, right down there in Carbondale. Damn right I did. I'll tell you anything you want to know; philosophy, science, politics, history, all that shit. That's right. You know where Carthage would be on the map today?

AS: Yeah, I want to know that, too.

LD: I'll bet you do.

AS: Alright, tell me. North Africa somewhere.

LD: That's right. North Africa.

AS: You're not gonna tell me now, right?

LD: I'm gonna tell you. I just want to know if you got the answer. I know my history.

AS: Well, go ahead then. Tell me.

LD: Alright, I'm gonna tell you. Carthage is where the nation of Tunisia is today.

AS: Tunisia?

LD: That's right.

AS: Hannibal was a black man.

LD: Damn right, he was a black man.

AS: You know what the Carthaginians used to do with their mercenaries once they had no use for them?

LD: I know what they did. I'm a black man. I know all about slavery.

Lefty Dizz and Detroit Junior

AS: But you're Chicago born, right?

LD: That's right. I was born right here in Chicago. But I learned the blues from those people from Mississippi. At least I hope I learned the blues. I think I play them. But I learned them blues from those people from Mississippi.

AS: And you play some blues, too.

LD: Ain't no rain, blood, shit or flood gonna stop me from playing the blues. Cause as sure as my name is Lefty Dizz, that's the way it is. Can you dig it?

AS: Ain't no what?

LD: Ain't no rain, blood, shit or flood. That covers just about everything, don't it?

AS: Just about. I like that. But what happened to that beautiful lady you were sitting with here at the bar earlier?

LD: What lady?

AS: That real pretty dark haired one.

LD: When was that?

AS: Just before the last set.

LD: Hey, listen, just because you see me talkin' to some woman don't mean I'm out to make it with her. I got lots of women.

AS: I know. That's not what I meant. I was just wondering where she went because I didn't see her leave, and I was looking.

LD: You think I picked her up? Hell, I give away more women than most men get. I was just walking down the street and she spotted me. That's right. I give away more women than most men get. And you know why? Cause I'm out here seven nights a week, dig it. I'm always available, unless my woman is with me...and then I'm cool. I ain't after all these women. You think I chase all these women? I gave up that conquest shit when I was sixteen years old. That's right. Besides, I'm a married man. That's right. I got 34 kids, you know.

AS: What! 34 kids?

LD: You don't believe me, right?

AS: I believe you. I just think that's an awful lot of kids.

LD: I got three sets of twins, two sets of triplets, one set of...

AS: You know all their names?

LD: I got them all written down someplace.

AS: I'll bet you do.

LD: That's right.

Jimmy Johnson

King Azure Blue

America is crumbling! The economy is failing! Nobody cares. The new silver dollar currently issued is the size of a quarter...and isn't even silver. The Mayor's office, in charge of special events, would have held Chicago's 2nd Annual Summer Music Festival in a sewer except they found Navy Pier to be suitably larger.

Music industry celebrities from all over the country have invaded the city. Every night is like a magic show of spontaneous rhythm and blues. Like a vast unofficial Mardi Gras. And to emphasize the season the city has found itself locked in the throes of a classical midwest hot and humid August with tremendous electrical storms occurring nightly. King azure blue. The quiet expectations of a storm.

Saturnal greased lightning in your electronic dry wall. How's your glazed face, fella? How's your spiked cinder heels? How's your Duke Tumato 3rd person singular second set? Sexy lady and only sixteen years old, long brushed eyelash, knocking them dead at the summerfest, dancing before the band like some mythical harem queen.

Jimmy Johnson, headlining the weekend at the Kingston Mines, is red hot. Then in walk The Pointer Sisters, drawn like a magnet to this late night jamming blues house. In walks Willy Dixon, the man who wrote half the blues songs sung these days. Straw Panama bowler, tall stout and prominent, humble man of deserved letters. Walks up on stage and got it on like nobody's business. Everyone jumping into a back-up chorus for the Man, Mr. Dixon. Koko Taylor, Willy Dixon's unofficial female spiritual co-existant, arrives from down the street...Wang Dang Doing it.

Besides the City Municipality sponsored Musicfest down at Navy Pier, The Chicago Blues Association would like to invite you to their all-star fund raising benefit Sunday evening at the Kingston Mines – Chicago Blues Center. Like a who's who in the very nature of the craft. From the west coast, ice pickin' Albert Collins, and Addie. From Houston, Texas, Lavelle White. From Chicago, Willie Dixon, Koko Taylor, Aron Burton, Lefty Dizz, Big Time Sarah, Casey Jones, Jimmy Johnson, Syl Johnson, Leroy Brown, Eddie Clearwater...no rehearsals, just the greatest spontaneous live song and guitar blues show on earth.

Thunder crashing in the heavens out doors. The back room of the Mines is a foot deep in pouring down rain. There is so much static electricity and humidity in the air the cash register won't work without delivering the user an electric shock! And it's the first night of the full moon. Lots of yelling between the celebrations and trying to keep the emotional overloads here at a minimum.

Meanwhile, a reliable lady of astrological knowledge reports that Neptune is messing with Virgo, which means it is a bad time for lovers. And the heart breaks demand you'll have to make it on your own.

"Gonna tie you up," sings Duke Tumato, "then hand you the rope."

"Baby, I give you money three or four times a day."

Suppose to be this way till October. Well, we all knew that.

A.C. Reed *Albert Collins*

Albert Collins

Living In Paradise

Having Albert Collins and Jimmy Johnson together on stage is like having two trains go at each other down the same track. They never stop gaining on each other and there ain't no collisions. Lots of friends waving from the windows. There is no way to know for sure. There is just so much any one man can pay attention to.

A.C. Reed *Albert Collins*

Albert Collins   *Aron Burton*

Larry Burton   *A.C. Reed*   *Albert Collins*   *Casey Jones*   *Aron Burton*

Squeezing The Tail Of The Law

At 2 a.m. nobody bothered to close the doors, even though the Kingston Mines is now a 2 o'clock bar. At 3 a.m. the band stopped to take a break. There was an argument then on whether to close the place or not, because being open all night with the full house lights on, the front doors wide open, people coming in and out, was unwise considering just two weeks earlier the club was raided and attention was brought to the fact that the late night license was gone. And being open now after 2 a.m. is like breaking the law. And the police might come again, just to check us out. The counter argument went, "Be cool, man. There's nothing to worry about."

I was standing out front with Cindy, one of the under age waitresses, when the same cop who led the charge last time, a Sergeant Nolan, Chicago Police Department, pulled up to the Mines again. This time with squad cars, paddy wagons, evidence control units, the works. "Ok, folks, everybody freeze. Don't touch that shot glass, lady." License violation time. Not like in the movies, at all. No arrests were made. Just photographs of evidence and forms to be filled out and signed by the management, just to get your ass in court.

The Aron Burton Blues Band, featuring "The Spoon" Jimmy Witherspoon

A Pair Of Neon Eyebrows

I get a call from The Lizard. He's out on bail again. I don't ask him what he was in for. His image, probably. But he's out now and wants to meet me later for drinks and take me to see his new wave rock group he is currently producing, a group called Toe Rot. Sounds fascinating, I tell him. My plan is to cruise past the Mines first, to see if they are open. They are. Good to hear. I have a drink there just to hang out a bit, find out the court date for the license violation won't be for a month or so, and that business can go on as usual. A license violation does not necessarily mean license suspension, though it could. Then cut out for the punk side of town. Which is just down the street on the other end of the Lincoln Avenue strip. *Where the Lizard lurks.* Sells leather whips out of an old bicycle powered ice cream cart on weekends. He's an hour and a half late, and I'm pretty stewed already by the time he shows up. I can't help myself. He shows up with a Scottish guy who is wearing clear plastic kilts and a set of neon eyebrows.

"Cute," I tell him.

"Get with it," the Scot tells me back.

"I will, but just remember, talent is not enough. In order to make it in the real world, you still have to be pretty good."

"I know, I know," he says. "You think all us guys ever do is repeat our three little chords and walk around pigeon toed all night, right?"

"No, that's not all I think, you plastic petty coat. Next year the new draft legislation."

We have a drink together. Lizard introduces me to Jerome Sala, the young punk poet who gets up each set and reads several of his works on stage before the band comes on. Tells me he thinks he's somewhat of a whore because he does it for free...to free his generation...and to develop an enlightened audience for his punker band artists...and that he's the only punk poet worth reading...even though he's not published. I kinda like this one. Maybe because he doesn't wear the fashionable half-wit look on his face. And despite his constant yelling, "FAG, FAG, FAG, FAG!" in my ear.

"Who gives a shit," I tell him back, "...if you wanna wear band-aides on your leatherette underwear. Support these guys, but keep your standards high."

I have to leave. That last song, a serious ballad about beer nuts, wired into the same lobotomy hyped up disco beat, is just too much for me. The plastic kilt with the eyebrows offers to lend me his leg braces to help me learn how to walk funny. Thanks a lot. I hobble down to the diner down the street to have a bowl of soup and watch the blurs run down the sports page.

One Head Out The Door

The coast is clear. A week goes by and all that has occurred at the Mines is a reduction in activity. A lull in the action. Possibly, the calm before the storm. Like something startling; the realization that nothing can be happening. The work crew aimlessly pacing the floors. If this was a Hollywood action film the hero would now be yelling his orders and pushing his people around in a constructive effort to defend themselves. Fortify the town. "Let's paint the place!" is suggested. It is the second week of the Chicagofest, and the blues stage down at Navy Pier is running continuous acts from noon til midnight everyday, including many of Doc's acts, to record crowds. And hurting the nightclub business. Yet, the feeling is that the big excitement will, in the end, develop new customers for the nightclub owners and eventually help business. But, either way, one slow week coupled with two less hours of the late night trade, per day, is putting the squeeze on Doc. Who, in response, raises the price of drinks.

At two minutes before the hour of 2 a.m., Friday night, just five days since the notice of licence violation, the Kingston Mines is busy selling drinks. So what, right? Who cares? Fuck the cops. Post a doorman outside. If you see the cops coming, signal and lock the doors quick. You know, just like in the movies. The idea of risking your nightclub on the gamble that you can do an extra twenty dollars or so during the final ten minutes of the night boggles the senses. A bad bet if I ever heard one. Granted, the rent must be paid. And Doc pays an enormous rent. But this, "Let's put it all on the line... Let's see what you guys are made of, campaign..." You get better odds at a Dog Show. And at a Dog Show they're just playing for ribbons.

Sally Sohn

The Fact Of The Matter Is

The fact of the matter is, the more Doc has the more Doc spends. And Doc *always* spends more than he has. It is a game of catch up. Always has been. Just like the city's baseball club, the Chicago Cubs. Except the Cubs never win in the end. But then, the Mines hasn't won anything, as yet, either. Nor is it the end. Nor is winning as important as how you win, or how you play. And we should keep in mind that losing is just a part of the play. Herman Franks, the Cubs' manager, would agree with me. Herman Franks concedes games. I'm sure of it. He doesn't *want* to win every game. That wouldn't make any sense to him. I don't know why. Maybe he has a bad heart and the excitement of winning everyday would be too much for him. Or maybe he thinks a ball club is *suppose* to lose games. Keeps the pressure of success at a reasonable level. I think ball clubs are supposed to lose games too, though not on purpose. Three days of no excitement at the Mines is like having a pig over for poker. Even nothing going wrong stands out as some kind of omen. I think Herman Franks has gotten to me.

Saturday night, August 11, 1979. At midnight tonight the Chicagoland area is suppose to be bombarded by 820 tons of spectacular meteor debris from the tail of the passing comet Perseids. A cosmic tribute of light raining down from the heavens in the northeast corner of a very clear sky. As if the god Jupiter was sneezing sparklers.

Midnight came and nothing happened.

Perseids must have cancelled out.

Carey Bell at ChicagoFest

Mary Hobbs and Phil Guy

On The Price Of A Mythology

Customer: I have to get used to these prices. I mean they don't charge this much for a drink at the Playboy Club.

Bartender: Ya, but then the Playboy Club doesn't have this much to offer.

Customer: Hey, can I get me some coke here?

Bartender: Sure, you can get some coke here.

Customer: (Making nasal gestures to his preferred definition of the word, coke.) Yeah, I mean can I get me some coke?

Bartender: Sure you can, but it's very expensive.

Customer: That's alright. (Elbowing his buddy sitting next to him. Both of them all smiles.) It's been a long time since I had me some good coke.

Bartender: Well, you can get it here. But, like I said, it's very expensive.

Customer: Well, what do I have to do, and how much?

Bartender: Well, first you have to tip the bartender.

Customer: Oh yeah? How much?

Bartender: Twenty.

Customer: Oh yeah?

Queen Sylvia Embry

Bartender: That's right.

Customer: Alright. (Reluctantly reaching for some money in his pocket.) And then what?

Bartender: And then you go to the airport and buy yourself a ticket to Columbia.

Customer: Ok. I get it.

Pie In The Sky

The story is that this carpetbagger son of a suburbanite, Bruce Iguana, owner of Reptile Records, has been buying up Doc's acts with a promise of fame and fortune. But what he has been paying these bands, for an album produced on his label, is a flat $500. Call it old fashion business. Or call it highway robbery. For his $500, Iguana gets everything; the copyrights to the music and songs recorded, full distribution rights, radio residuals, and a giant loop hole out of paying the recording artists any royalties on copies sold by stating in his contracts that royalties are only paid to the recording artist after the album has sold a certain number of copies. A number that will never be reached. What Iguana does offer the bands he signs to his label is a respected and good paying tour through Europe, a tour that might pay a band leader as much as several thousand dollars per week. But this is where Iguana makes his biggest money. And this is how he does it. After he's sold as many copies of an album as he can in this country, he resells the entire package to a European label, for an enormous price, along with the group "on tour" to help promote sales on that continent. It's a pretty good deal if you can get away with it, and Iguana seems to be doing so. The point is that Iguana has no competition. Reptile Records is the only label in town recording these guys.

There is another hitch to the deal. As it turns out, Doc's only real competition in the area is a club owned in part by no other than this Iguana. And, in exchange for these no fault, no royalties recording contracts, Iguana expects these bands to play at his club exclusively, and not at Doc's. And you have to play at one club or the other. You are either with him or you're not. So in order for Doc to be a simple nightclub owner he has to compete, not only with the other clubs around, but with the local recording company and booking agent. Maybe start his own syndicate of promotional events, world wide, just to avoid getting squeezed out of the market. Or, as been suggested, maybe send over a couple thugs to blow Iguana back to Peoria, or wherever he came from.

The irony is that more than half of the big blues acts playing the northside today were developed in conjunction with Doc at the Kingston Mines. And it is not until these bands begin getting good audience response and a solid following that the competition comes in with their pie in the sky contracts, with restrictions to where, and where not to play.

Also, the Environmental Protection Agency, on orders from "Downtown" has twice this week written Doc tickets for violations under the heading of "Noise Pollution." Can this be possible on a street in the big city that happens to be lined with taverns, saloons, and nightclubs? Three days of silence and then it's back to the range war. Except I didn't know there was a range war. Or, for that matter, who the range war was with.

Nuke Me Baby
(Nuke Me All Night Long)

Chicago, the city where Elizabeth Kubler-Ross discovered life after death. In a laboratory, just feet away from where scientists, 40 years earlier, invented the atomic bomb!

Nuke me baby, nuke me all night long

Radiation.

If I got to go

I want to go out with a glow,

Radiation.

There are complaints of strange sores developing in the nasal cavities of the local inhabitants. Myself, being a local inhabitant, can attest to the confirmation of these reports. We are told it is due to excessive pollutants in the atmosphere. We have three alternatives. Get used to it. Stop breathing. Or get out of town.

Harvey Mandel, local big guy on the rock guitar and roll scene, is up on stage with Addie, Aron Burton, and Dimestore Fred. It is Addie's first night as headliner. Nolan, the sergeant who keeps showing up at 2 a.m. to bust the place, has been sitting on the corner with two paddy wagons all night. The audience is huge and celebrating the inauguration of jamming as a true art form. Addie has needed her own night for a long time to stretch out and really show her stuff, and tonight is certainly her night. And with Harvey Mandel to accompany her, and to have on stage to bounce her riffs off of. A truly explosive scene.

And yet, I can't stop the business concepts from creeping into my thoughts. And they should not be in my thoughts. And yet they are. Like, what would this place look like cleaned up? Or, imagine what a half million could do for the back room, the ailing old equipment, or the roof. None of my business, really. I should be concerned with the cult myth of the blues, and the no myth reality. These guys don't need a myth. Because these guys are all too real and just simply play. Although, a good myth might be good for business... Leave it alone, because business has a way of reducing the magic. Let the management contend with the business. Because music is magic, and magic should not be leaned upon. Forget the business. It is the magic I should be after. And the magic is too intangible, and tends to simply vanish... at the mere mention of... business.

"Oh yeah, I know Chicago. That's where a man danced with his wife."
A customer

Aron Burton

Squared Black Holes

After hours and everyone is gone. All the faces and jamboree. All the talk. The bar wiped down and things put away. The beer cooler restocked for the following day. Doc is the only man I know who can dump all the change from the cigarette machine out on a table and count up all the nickels, dimes, and quarters, as much as $400, or more, while at the same time keep a constant dialogue about who's playing where, making what, fucking who, changes in the program, and so forth. "$48.50. There you go." Except tonight, while Doc is counting the change he is mumbling under his breath the name, "Nolan. Sgt. Nolan. We gotta do something to get that guy off our ass."

Instead of waiting for me to finish up some notes, Doc and Mary pick up a couple of flashlights and go through the rear of the club and up the back stairs to the third floor to inspect a support beam for the roof that is water damaged from the leak in the roof and failing. They are gone for a long time and I am sitting around waiting for them to come down and let me out. The door is locked. I walk around the room examining the after hours mess and wreckage left over for the porter in the morning to deal with, the smells and tarnished colors covering the walls, the stage... the shag carpet covering the stage — totally assaulted. Has a science fiction desolated look to it. As if someone fought a battle there. One fan working on top of the old piano up front keeps the napkins and other assorted debris caught in the stage shag rug moving. As if the city were deserted. Evacuated. All

The Albert King Blues Band

the junk left behind. Carefully blowing in the wind. Giving the feeling that the world is incredibly dank. That the lights should not be raised here. That the lights, in fact, should be lowered. (Scene fades with the hollow hammered out music sounds echoing in the background. Camera pans to the dance floor.)

I walk out back into the unused horse stable huge cavern of a room and stare up at the tall ceiling; large shafts built into the network of ceiling supports, probably meant for elevators or spaces to throw hay down from the upper lofts, when the back room was a stable. (General Pershing, it has been said, once kept a stable of his cavalry mounts here enroute to his campaign in Mexico.) The shafts so dark and deep, as if they had no end, as if they could be squared black holes in a squared black sky, or wells pointed in the wrong direction. I call out to Doc and Mary and hear my voice echo back. Then after a second or two Mary calls out and I hear them coming down the steps. There is no talk about the support beam problem, or the roof. Now there is just a sign to change on the billboard out front advertising the show for tomorrow night.

But Dank Is Just A Word

But dank is just a word. The roof caving in on a full house weekend crowd is a whole other matter. It has rained nearly every night, so far, this August. Terrific lightning storms creating vast silhouettes in the sky of tremendous grey black storm clouds bursting full with water. Completely and visually spellbinding. The thunder moves across the city in waves of loud rumbles, followed by earth shattering claps that tend to jar your senses. Then the lightning comes. As if the world was under attack. Rays of brilliant light flashes. Everywhere. Taking over. Total surrender. The charge of particles in the air, in your very blood coursing through your veins, caused by that next lightning shock. You forget you're getting wet watching this natural wonder occur in the sky.

The weather bureau is advising people to stop using their appliances. I don't know why, but it's storm related.

Then the rain comes, slapping down in sheets. Hardly any wind at all, yet the air gets violently moved about caused by the down pouring rain. Then the rain stops and there is just a mist frozen in the drizzling haze, a kind of granite grey dampness that hangs in the air and remains there for hours, or minutes, until the next blast comes. A kind of physical wet explosion stays in the air and refuses to settle. And this has been going on for days. Meanwhile, Doc's roof is disintegrating.

Eddie Clearwater

London During The Blitz

The Eddie Clearwater Band, Lavelle White, Addie, Leroy Brown, and Dimestore Fred are all on stage, and the Mines is completely flooded. Outside it is storming like crazy. The sewer in the back room is clogged and the water that is hailing down from the shafts in the ceiling and the holes in the roof is three or four inches deep. And the water has stopped rising only because it hit the level high enough to start pouring into the front music room. People are dancing in puddles. One of the weekend waitresses, named Julie, explains to me the contours of the concrete floor and how the water level in her section has reached ankle deep proportions. She orders from the bar two bourbons on the rocks and a package of Lifesavers. At first I think she is kidding because the band is playing and carrying on, and there is a capacity house dancing as though everything was completely normal. Maybe the room is a bit more humid than usual, but then there is a storm raging outdoors. Several of the waitresses have abandoned their stations and can be found mingling with the customers in the standing room only area in the rear of the room by the bar.

Meanwhile, Mary, Little Cindy, and Barbara are on the roof in the midst of another great lightning thunder storm armed with only a bucket of tar, a roll of tar paper, two hammers and a squeegee. Their mission is to patch up holes. Keep the ship afloat. Outer space battle front heroics. Barbara comes down from the roof soaking wet. Crazed particle smile on her face. Her arms tarred to the elbows. She was applying the tar to the roof with her hands!

I'm having a hard time registering all this. First of all, Eddie Clearwater is better than ever, possibly giving the best performance I have ever seen him give. Every song is getting full powerhouse treatment. The audience is wild and right with him. And he's using everyone in his show to choreograph his hits, disappears to somewhere for a moment, then jumps back on stage in a new, even wilder costume; a red leather suit with an orange satin cape. Looks like a frogman with mushroom tendencies. They won't let Lavelle White off stage after two encores. Even cool Leroy Brown is hot. Everything is wet. I gasp at my sudden realization that I am suppressing catastrophe. Water is now dripping from the ceiling everywhere. The biggest threat is Doc's complex electrical wiring system which consists of extension cords running everywhere, connecting everything. I tell Julie that if she notices everyone go suddenly very still with funny smiles on their faces, to freeze! Don't touch anything!

All sorts of images start coming to me. Subterranean cities. The Titanic. London during the blitz. There is a certain madness in the air, highly charged. Due to the intense electrical storm raging outside, all the dampness in the room, the hot band, the drink, the fruitlessness of trying to keep your clothes crisp and clean, topped with the absurdity and surrealistic charm of just being in this room, under these conditions, with all these people, and having a good time despite the chaos of water dripping everywhere, puddles on your dance floor, total sensory weirdness.

I begin to think, what a show! How could anyone possibly forget a night like this? Bits and small pieces of plaster begin falling from the ceiling where the water has been leaking through. The roof is finally coming down! People are hugging and kissing anyway, on their feet and dancing. Making love in the face of apocalypse. Dancing in the face of certain doom. Apocalypse Now, Baby! Right here at the Kingston Mines! The band refuses to stop playing. It is past closing time but neither Doc nor Mary can stop the show. The room is simply out of control.

News Spreads Fast

News spreads fast. Twenty minutes after opening the next night the place is packed. A guy from out of town asks the bartender and myself what the atmosphere of the club is like. I don't know exactly what to say and begin to laugh. "Well, I'll tell you," the bartender says leaning over a beer, "after last night we're all just kinda happy to still be here."

Laura Pellegrino

Moose Walker

Like A Hot Balloon In A Cold Cut Store

    Days come and disappear. Take a night off to rewire circuits, bionic brain chips, water the plants, stay home, turn on the radio, listen to the Cub baseball highlights, write some letters, scratch around through some half read books. Take a walk... and buy a newspaper. The big headlines read, "SOVIET COSMONAUTS RETURN TO EARTH AFTER 175 DAYS OF TOILET TRAINING AND DIRTY SOX." Sounds like an editorial. "We understand their mission to have consisted of rigorous exercises in patience control, forward and lateral motionlessness, occasional button pushing and long stares into deep dark space." Zen Cosmonauts.

    There are still heavy clouds in the sky and lightning blasts about every four hours... as if the city were under siege... thunder clouds roll in like hot balloons in a cold cut store... then explode over the city. Trench coat and wide brim hat vibes. Covert strolls in the park. A great city washing.

    What Doc did to save the remaining portions of the ceiling from falling down was to construct a wide trough like gutter out of a pile of old doors and sheets of heavy plastic, like a simple aqueduct on the second floor over the music room in order to channel off the rain water towards the rear of the building where Doc finally got the sewer cleared so the water has a place to go other than in through the rear door of the club.

After a long coffee at the Seminary Restaurant on Lincoln and Fullerton I walk east up the street on Lincoln to the Mines to pay a visit to Dimestore Fred, who is there cleaning up the place, which is what Fred does to supplement his income. I often go in early after a good night in order to discuss my hangovers with Dimestore Fred, who is good to discuss these topics with. Laughs a lot. But neither one of us was hung over, and the topic of conversation was the large puddle of catsup on the sidewalk in front of the Mines I noticed on my way in.

There were no bits or pieces of glass surrounding the large puddle, though we supposed there should have been in order to account for it's origin. But the main problem was not how it got there, but how it was going to disappear. Fred didn't want to clean it up, though it would be his job to, and I couldn't even consider it. Nevertheless, something had to be done. So Fred decided to lay next to it and pretend he was dead while I look over his mashed catsup head and feint hysteria. Didn't work on the first girl passing by, a young tall black girl who caught the whole act from a distance down the street, and as she slowed towards our stage, stopped and said, "Catsup." While we were rolling in laughter and hailed her passage through. Until the next victim, a fat already agitated white woman who did not see the humor and when I told her Fred got hit by a fireplug, she said, "Then call the Fire Department!" And scurried off. And there was more laughter due from the fact she took our joke seriously. So seriously that during a following intent to distract a passerby, a Fire Department Ambulance Unit, lights flashing, pulled up stopping traffic and, "Oh boy, Fred. Get up, man." There was a lawyer chasing the ambulance in a bright red sports car, kept calling us assholes, while Fred and I just stood there, slightly embarrassed, saying, "Sorry. Just a joke."

A Liquid Of Amber Substance

After dinner and a movie I decided to stop back at the Mines for a nightcap. Aron Burton and Casey Jones were playing and had just finished their set. People were up and about, at the bar for more drinks and walking in and out the front door. A James Cotton album came on. Aron Burton and Lavelle White were going out for a smoke. Stop and say hello… "Hey, how's it going… Alright." Casey Jones was fighting the ladies off at the bar. The band members are ordering drinks. Everything looking to be quite normal except for Doc, who had come in and was wandering around in a daze, and Mary who was passed out in a booth. Neither one of them had gotten any sleep the night before… up all night at the club celebrating Mary's 24th birthday, and both of them making the best of their time before they had to be downtown "in court" at the Daley Center Plaza to answer before the judge regarding an after hour bar owner license violation.

Doc was eager to tell the story. Shook his head once to keep himself awake, then got right into it. "We stopped and had breakfast first on our way downtown just to calm ourselves down, but by the time we got downtown we were so hyped out of it we ended up just leaving the car parked in front of that big rust red Picasso sculpture in the plaza right there on Clark Street. Then went up to court.

"The funny thing was, there were these representatives there from the Alderman's Office... That's right. What are they doing there? Including the Alderman's private secretary. I think her name is Linda something, a tall middle aged redhead. Maybe you know her. Linda something, real nervous and pushy. She comes up to me and tells me to sign in, right, which is the bailiff's job, first of all, and not hers. So I told her I'd have my lawyer do that for me when he gets here. Which she doesn't like hearing. Like I'm not suppose to have a lawyer or something. Very weird.

"So we all fan out through the courtroom, which is relatively empty, and take our seats until the lawyer shows up... Who's in pretrial conference with the judge. I have this very good lawyer by the way. Cost me $750 for one hour's work.

"So the lawyer shows up, and Sgt. Nolan is sitting there in the front row. And the judge shows up. And the bailiff swears us all in. Then the lawyer cuts right to Nolan.

"The lawyer says, 'Did you see any money exchange hands?' And Nolan says, 'No.' And the lawyer says, 'Did you see any people in the nightclub other than employees?' And Nolan says, 'No.'

"The judge is giving Nolan dirty looks now. Then the lawyer says, 'Was there anyone sitting at the bar by the two drinks you photographed as your evidence?' 'No.' 'You have described the contents of the two glasses on the bar to contain an amber substance. Can you describe more clearly to the court what you mean by an amber substance?' Nolan says, 'A liquid of amber color.'

"The judge leans over his big desk and looks down at Nolan and says, 'You understand, Sgt. Nolan, that urine may also be classified under your definition of a liquid of amber substance.'

"Wow, really knocked me out, the judge saying that. Then Nolan says, 'Yes, I know that, your Honor.' Then the judge says, 'I think we'll just have to dismiss this case... Case Dismissed.' The whole thing took no more than three minutes. Thrown out of court... And when we got downstairs the car didn't even have a ticket."

Frank Pellegrino

People leave here feeling good. They don't leave feeling introspective.

A Moral In The Story

You look hard as the months roll by for a single thread that can be used to weave the whole summer together, a sense of higher meaning, a trend in the music, possibly a broader spiritual consistency in which to embody all the above stories under. A moral in the story. A moral does not exist. Everything gets tried, yet only what works out well succeeds.

The room gets seized by a Bo Diddley beat. It comes from out of nowhere after a slow blues followed by a long quiet pause. It begins to build in intensity. Everyone awakes to the sound of it's beat. Everyone nodding their heads and moving their bodies as if dancing in their seat. Then up, springing onto the stage Aron Burton grabs the microphone and calls for a roar of applause for an old Otis Rush song entitled, "Chickenhead." And the audience starts calling out, "Chickenhead! Chickenhead! Chickenhead!" Which goes something like this:

> *Daddy told me*
>   *On his dying bed*
> *Said give up your heart*
>   *but don't lose your head*
> *You came around girl*
>   *and what did I do*
> *I lost my heart*
>   *and my head went too*

Little girl, little girl
    you sure can cook
Little girl, little girl
    you got me hooked
When you cook that chicken
    & save me the head
I should be working
    but I'm home in bed

Dreaming about you
    every night and every day
I love that girl
    I love them chickenheads

(chorus)
Without your love
    I can't go on
The feeling I have for you
    is much too strong
Let me in, let me in
    let me in, let me ease on in

My love for you
    is so gosh darn strong
Like the Mississippi River
    rolls on and on
Loving you
    is a dog gone crime
I'm sitting in jail
    on a flat 99
Dreaming about you
    every night and every day
I love that girl
    I love them chickenheads

(chorus)
Wait a minute
　Some like the breast
Some like the leg
　Some like the wing
But save me the head

Love them chicken heads
　Crazy about them chickenheads

There is nothing silly about the blues. It is a good time music with no bullshit... Well, maybe a little bullshit. A hot drummer in the Fenton Robinson Band, named Gates, said, "All you can go for, as a blues musician, is perfection." Then he named a few musicians he thought had reached perfection.

If there is a moral necessary for the story, let it be this — This is the entertainment business. People leave here feeling good. They don't leave here feeling introspective.

Lavelle White... making the flowers grow.

Like The Ancient Run Of The Caribou

Several weeks go by. Then, suddenly, you can feel the season change. You can't see it yet, but you can feel it like you can feel anything. You can sense it in the air. The feeling manifests itself in a desire to re-examine your last year's autumn wardrobe. For instance, yesterday I woke up and right after coffee began oiling up my high leather boots. Several employees have gone back to school, each leaving for their own respective university.

You can feel the urge for moving. Maybe California for the winter... Blues Festival down in Mexico City in January... Then NYC for the spring. Take the Amtrak. Leave all the old clothes in the closet. Change is everywhere.

Doc and Mary got formally engaged. Best wishes and congratulations. A spontaneous celebration occurred. The James Cotton Band, plus Fenton Robinson and his band, came by and played all night behind Johnny Dollar, Lavelle White, Little Bobby Nealy, and Addie. The compressor on the beer cooler went out and all the bottled beer had to be red shifted into styrofoam tubs filled with ice.

Dimestore Fred, that night, was playing at a far northside club called Biddy Mulligan's, where after hours the manager of the club, a fellow named Chip Covington, took it upon himself to wreck his place. He started by first throwing bar stools across the room, then graduated to tables and chairs, and then topped it all off with a barrage of assorted whiskeys and beer bottles. According to Fred, Covington encouraged the band members and the bar crew to participate in the wrecking of his establishment. Though, knowing Dimestore Fred, it might have been the other way around. Either way, Fred told me that by the time he left that place, he was covered from head to toe in bitters and Galiano.

Or maybe its the dark clouds over the city every day and night for the past solid month that makes you think that the summer is nearing its end. Or maybe the lightning storms every night are trying to tell us something entirely different. "Yellow Fever on the Moon." One wonders what perils awaits the Mines this fall. "Earthquake '79." "A Brigade of Commando Rockers." Surely, nothing that couldn't be dealt with, at the Kingston Mines, triumphantly... even in its darkest days.

Phil Guy

End Of The Season

The day after Labor Day and the streets are deserted. No traffic on the streets, not even cars on the big busy intersections. Doc explains it will be like this for a month or so before the new season begins that will lead right into New Years.

I get to the club early and find Dimestore Fred sitting on stage, microphone and harp in hand, blowing along with an old Howling Wolf record, playing the same song over and over until he gets it right.

It is the end of the season. I look around and inspect the equipment; beat up, parts taped together. The air conditioners were never repaired. Both refrigerators and the ice machine are out. The air is hot and resinous. I notice the soda gun is broken, and hanging on it's little plastic hook like a torn up toy robot whose head got slightly knocked astray exposing its springs and wires. I wonder how that happened. I pick it up and test out the remaining fragments. I press the coke button and syrup shoots out the top of the gun squirting me in the face, while the soda water sprays out from the bottom. I figure out you have to hold the top disconnected part down with your free hand to get both syrup and soda jets going in the same direction.

I hang the limp gun back onto its hook and watch the soda start shooting on and off across the room, all by itself. I grab the gun back but it won't stop shooting until I slam it a couple of times on the bar. I am convinced our sole purpose in life, on this planet, is to evolve. (What are you doing here? Evolving.)

The heavy clouds and rain storms have finally broke, and the sky is once again clear, crisp and blue. Really lovely days now. Like an early Indian Summer. "Migration Time."

Doc has planned a giant Blues Extravaganza for Sunday. Begins in the afternoon and goes straight on until closing. An all day affair. On a full moon night. Maybe even an eclipse. But the place has got to get itself back together again for that one big show. Big all-star revue. Then call the real repairmen in, right. Meanwhile, scratching around for more tape.

Michael Coleman, Lavelle White, Ray Moyena, Nick Charles, Moose Walker

No Breaks

Doc's Blues Extravaganza began at two o'clock in the afternoon, and went straight on until two in the morning. And there were so many performers scheduled to be on the show that there wasn't even time between sets for breaks. No breaks. And only two of the regular employees, either through sheer determination or physical strength alone, made it through the entire shift. And that was the waitress, Sally Sohn, who late that night accused her legs of being fragments of a running hallucination... but who was working her way through school and was behind enough on her tuition payments to warrant the school to threaten her with dismissal, and sought the twelve hour shift as her escape hatch to freedom. The other employee being little Barbara Ann Daniel, the runner, stocker, dish washer, and do all, who despite her classic Assyrian dark eyes and good looks, was not designed to tire, and would, rather, simply work than not. All the other employees either collapsed, or had to quit. But then, no one expected the concert to draw such a crowd.

The event was set up as a benefit for a non-profit group who had organized as a coalition to keep their housing unit rents down, and had sold 400 advanced tickets, though they didn't expect half that number to show. Instead, the benefit drew senior citizens in wheelchairs, whole families including their children. It was like a big wedding party... sans the circle dance and pastries... with kids shooting plastic toothpicks through soda straws at each other, while all the old folks got drunk.

And what a day and night for music. There must have been 50 or 60 of Chicago's finest blues musicians, in all, on stage throughout the concert. Occasionally the bandstand would make a complete change in personnel, for instance, like when Aron Burton and Casey Jones came on and did their regular set, accompanied by Larry Burton on lead guitar and A.C. Reed on saxophone. Or, when Carey Bell's band came on, accompanied, later in the set, by Carey's entire family.

But still, it was Carey Bell you have to talk about. And Carey was explosive. Because you have to understand that Carey Bell can pick on a mouth harp the way Jimmy Johnson can pick on a Fender. Let's you know there's still some wood involved. There was one special moment, if I had a camera with me, I could have caught Carey Bell suspended in the air, for an unnaturally long moment, the tensions created so great, both feet off the ground, his one free hand spread wide like the sun, up close before his face, like some kind of Kung Fu Blues, eye to eye in perfect concentration with his son, Laury Bell, both minds glued together.

How the concert was set up for the most part was like this: Fenton Robinson's band served as house band, and opened up the afternoon, with Fenton, featuring Johnny Dollar and Lavelle White. And then for the better part of the concert people would come on in a virtual stream of guest appearances, endless show stoppers, and constantly changing combinations of musicians on the stage. But there were people brought up as guests that I had never seen before, from as far away as Vancouver. Roy Hytower did a set. Then Lonnie Brooks brought in some of his Bayou Lightning. Big Time Sarah got on. Fenton Robinson and Jimmy Johnson did their sets together. Lavelle White made the flowers grow. Lefty Dizz was away touring Europe.

I remember the way the night eventually ended. The band just stopped. They were all sitting down, anyway. That's it folks. Got to go. Thank you. Have a good night. Drive home safely. And come see us again.

Albert King

Epilogue

So now it's ten years later, and reportedly, the economy of America is still failing. More disasters have occured in atomic power plants, and scientists have discovered serious holes in the heavens. We've elected new presidents and waged new wars. We've been exposed to secret weapons, pestilence, disease, you name it. Yet, business at the Kingston Mines couldn't be better.

Record crowds challenge the Mines' service capacity on a nightly basis. New bands have sprung up, while the great older bands keep getting greater. Doc, somehow, found a way to take ownership of the building at the new Kingston Mines, thus eliminating the problem of cheap, greedy, irresponsible landlords who refuse to keep their buildings in repair. Talk has it there might even be a second Mine opening in the near future.

Punk music has since gone the way of the rain forest, with rap music soon to follow. Yet, the blues remains undaunted, solid, regenerative, surviving the ages, supplying its followers and fans with a nightly cabaret. And this will continue, because in the words of Doc Pellegrino, "There are a lot more parties and good times to be had."

Amen to that.

Lefty Dizz, end of set

Book design by

**DOUBLE CLICK
DESIGN WORKS**

Chicago

Front Cover:
Original Photo by D. Shigley
Image Processed by Tim Karczewski